Textbook B

READING MASTERY III

Siegfried Engelmann
Susan Hanner

SCIENCE RESEARCH ASSOCIATES, INC.

S R A ®

Chicago, Palo Alto, Toronto, Henley-on-Thames, Sydney

A Subsidiary of IBM

Textbook B

READING MASTERY III

Contents

LINDA AND KATHY ALONE ON AN ISLAND

Linda and Kathy Construct a Water Wheel 3 ● Setting the Water Wheel in Place 11 ● The Water Wheel Works 18 ● The Girls Have Fish for Dinner 25 ● Signaling for Help 30 ● The Girls Are Rescued 37

MORE ABOUT HOHOBOHO

The Scarred Words in the Word Bank 43 ● The Number with the Most Scars 47 ● Some Words Stop Fighting 52 ● Another Announcement Is Made 56 ● The Last Problem in the Word Bank Is Solved 62

THE STORY OF TROY

A Great War at Troy 86 ● The Great Wooden Horse 89

BERTHA AND HER NOSE

Bertha Has a Great Sense of Smell 96 ● Bonnie Gets a Job as an Investigator 102 ● Bonnie Tests Bertha's Talent 110 ● Bonnie and Bertha Go to the Oil Refinery 113 ● Bonnie and Bertha Meet Mr. Daniels 118 ● Bertha Tests Some Water 123 ● Bonnie and Bertha Make Up a New Plan 129 ● Inside a Hot Trunk 134 ● The Chief Listens to Bertha 140 ● Bertha Tests the Water 145

THE STORY OF ACHILLES

Achilles' Heel 152 ● The Greatest Soldier 158

ANDREW DEXTER'S DREAMS

Andrew Dexter Has Daydreams 229 ● Andrew Visits
Magnetic Research Company 236 ● Andrew Is a Changed
Person 241 ● Andrew Gets Fired 251 ● Andrew Meets
Denny Brock 258 ● The Titans Make Fun of Andrew
265 ● Andrew Kicks 270 ● Denny Gives Andrew a Job
277 ● Andrew Plays in His First Game 281 ● Andrew
Meets Smiling Sam 287 ● Andrew Begins to Change
293 ● Andrew Plays Harder 299 ● The Titans Play Harder
305 ● Andrew Leaves the Team 310 ● The Championship
Game 315 ● The End of the Game 321

THE TIME MACHINE

Eric and Tom Find a Time Machine 343 ● The
San Francisco Earthquake 352 ● Eric and Tom in Egypt
361 ● Eric and Tom Meet the King of Egypt 368 ● Eric
and Tom Leave Egypt 374 ● Eric and Tom in Greece
379 ● Forty Thousand Years Ago 386 ● Eric and Tom
in the City of the Future 392 ● Spain in 1491 400 ●
The Dog and the Time Machine 408 ● The Land of
the Vikings 415 ● Trying to Get Home 424 ● Concord
430 ● Home 440

LESSON 71

A

1	2	3	4
strength	containers	upstream	uphill
fought	poured	mind	waterfall
difficult	streambed	screeched	twice
gasoline	becoming	darted	pound
shallow	reason	angrily	hammer

5	6	7
startled	listening	**Vocabulary words**
constructing	kneeling	1. school of fish
kilograms	freely	2. straighten
tugging	kneeled	3. struggle
dull	glow	4. exhausted
		5. steeper
		6. supported
		7. solve

B Linda and Kathy Construct a Water Wheel Ⓐ

Linda and Kathy were not able to pull the net from the water when it was filled with fish. Ⓑ

Linda began to think of a way to solve this problem. She sat on the rocks near the edge of the ocean and thought. Waves rolled in and splashed against the rocks. The sun was very hot.

Suddenly, Linda jumped up and said, "I've got it." Ⓒ

Kathy was sitting on the edge of the rocks. She was so startled by Linda that she almost fell into the water.

"I've got it," Linda repeated. "We will construct a water wheel to pull the net out of the water." Ⓓ ✿ 2 ERRORS ✿

"How will we do that?" Kathy asked.

"I'll show you," Linda said. She took some of the boards from the crate. "These will make fine blades," she said. She found a small straight tree trunk on the beach. Linda said,

"This will make a good shaft. Now we'll nail the parts together."

"We don't have a hammer or nails," Kathy said.Ⓔ

Linda said, "We'll pull some nails from the crate and pound them straight if they are bent. Then we'll use flat rocks for hammers."Ⓕ

The job was not easy. The sisters pulled a lot of nails from the crate, but straightening them was difficult. Linda hit her fingers twice. That hurt.Ⓖ

But by the time the sun was beginning to hide in the palm trees that lined the beach, Linda and Kathy had made something that looked like this:Ⓗ

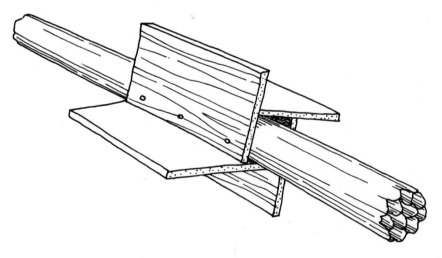

Linda said, "We've got to drag this water wheel up the stream until we come to a place where there is a little waterfall." Ⓘ

Dragging the water wheel was not easy. Kathy weighed 30 kilograms. Linda weighed 36 kilograms. The water wheel that they had constructed weighed 45 kilograms. Ⓙ

So they struggled and struggled. By the time they had dragged the water wheel to the stream, they were nearly exhausted. "Let's catch our breath," Kathy said. Ⓚ The blades of the water wheel had left deep tracks in the sand. But the worst part came when the girls started to follow the stream up into the hills. Moving the wheel uphill took great effort. Ⓛ Every few meters, the girls stopped to catch their breath. "How much farther do we have to go?" Kathy asked.

"I don't know," Linda snapped back angrily. Ⓜ She wasn't angry at Kathy. She was exhausted and didn't know where she would find enough strength to go on. Ⓝ

Kathy looked as if she was going to start crying. "Hey," Linda said. "I'm sorry. Let's sit down and rest for a while." So the girls rested.

Kathy sat on a rock in the middle of the stream and looked into the water. Ⓞ Schools of tiny fish darted this way and that way as if they were one body with one mind. Ⓟ Linda stood next to Kathy. The water came up to her knees. It was cold and clear. A few meters on either side of the stream was jungle. Leaves and vines fought for sunlight. Some leaves were nearly a meter long. Birds screeched. Ⓠ

"Time to move on," Linda said after a few minutes had passed.

Kathy shook her head and made a face to show that she was not very happy about getting back to work. Ⓡ

The farther they went upstream the more difficult it became to move the water wheel. Ⓢ The reason is that the streambed was becoming steeper and steeper. When the streambed becomes steeper, the water in the stream flows faster. When the water flows faster, it is harder to walk in the stream. And it is a lot harder to try to drag a heavy water wheel. Ⓣ

At last they came to a place where the streambed was almost flat. The water was deeper here. The stream made a little pool of water. And on the other side of the pool was a waterfall. The water tumbled down about three meters into the pool.

"This is the perfect place for the water wheel," Linda said. "Now all we have to do is set it up in that waterfall." Ⓤ ❀ 11 ERRORS ❀

LESSON 72

1	2	3
mosquito	poured	dull
unpleasant	containers	screeching
orange	gasoline	freely
beauty	glowing	listening
	shallow	

4	5	6
kneeled	forgotten	imagined
wrap	greased	thrashing
tugging	carton	unwound
carried	squeaking	jammed
liters		raw

7	8	9
burst	**Vocabulary words**	**Vocabulary words**
burn	**1.** imagine	**1.** trickle
pressed	**2.** force	**2.** signal
brighter	**3.** dam	**3.** tug
burning	**4.** gaps	**4.** supported

B

Liters

Here are facts about liters.

- A liter is used to measure liquids.(A) Here is a little cube that is one centimeter on all sides:

- A liter is made up of one thousand cubes of liquid.(B)
- A liter of fresh water weighs one kilogram.(C)
- Gasoline is sometimes sold by the liter.(D)
- Some cartons of milk hold about one liter.(E)

Here's a picture of a liter carton.(F)

Some containers in the picture hold one liter. Some containers hold less than one liter. Some containers hold four liters. The cat in the picture gives you a hint about which containers hold one liter. **G**

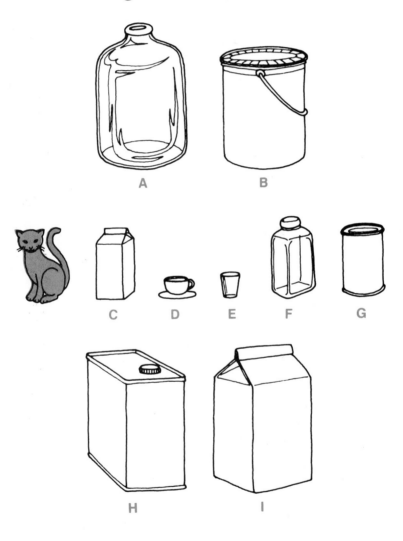

C
Setting the Water Wheel in Place Ⓐ

Putting a water wheel up in a waterfall is not an easy job because the water falls down with great force. Ⓑ One liter of fresh water weighs one kilogram. When that liter of water is dropping, it feels as if it weighs a lot more than one kilogram. Ⓒ When you jump down from a high place, you land very hard because you come down with great force. The waterfall that

Linda and Kathy found was dropping 20 liters of water every second.**(D)** If the girls tried to stick the water wheel under that falling water, they wouldn't be able to hold it in place.**(E)**

✿ 2 ERRORS ✿

Linda and Kathy climbed to the top of the waterfall. The water on the edge of the waterfall was very shallow, only about ten centimeters deep.**(F)** Linda said, "We'll pile big rocks right here on the edge to make a dam. That should hold the stream back while we put the water wheel in place." The picture on page 11 shows their dam.

They rolled four big rocks into the stream. Then they filled up the gaps between the big rocks with many smaller rocks. When they finished the dam, some water was still trickling through, but not very much. Quickly the girls pushed the water wheel into place.**(G)** The girls put a big rock under a blade of the water wheel to make sure that it wouldn't turn while they were fixing it.**(H)** The girls made a pile of heavy rocks under each end of the shaft. These rocks supported the shaft.**(I)** Linda greased the ends of the shaft with the milk from coconuts.**(J)** Then the girls pulled the rock out from under the blade of the water wheel. Finally, the girls removed some of the rocks from above the waterfall. Ⓚ The water tumbled down and hit the top blade of the water wheel with great force. The blade turned. The water hit the next board and pushed it down. The shaft turned faster and faster and faster. Ⓛ

As the girls watched their water wheel turning around and around, Kathy said, "That thing works well, but how is it going to help us pull our net from the water?"

Linda had almost forgotten the reason for constructing the water wheel.Ⓜ "We still have a lot of work to do," Linda said slowly.

"What kind of work?" Kathy said, making a face.Ⓝ

"We will have to make a long vine that will reach all the way from this water wheel to the beach."

"That's a long way," Kathy said. "It must be a kilometer or more."

Linda laughed. "No, it's much less than that. It just seems like a long way because we had to haul the water wheel up here.Ⓞ If you could see through the trees, you'd be able to see the beach right down there." Linda pointed.Ⓟ

The girls pulled vines from the trees and picked them up from the ground. They tied them together to make one long vine. They laid it along the streambed from the waterfall down to the beach. They tied the net to one end of the vine, and they carried the net into the water. Then Linda went back to the waterfall and picked up the other end of the vine. Kathy stayed on the beach. She was going to signal when the net was full of fish.Ⓠ Kathy was going to signal by tugging on the vine. Ⓡ When Linda felt the tug, she was going to wrap her end of the vine around the shaft of the water wheel. As the shaft turned and turned, it would pull more vine around the shaft. It would slowly pull the net toward the shore.

Linda went up the streambed and kneeled down next to the water wheel and waited. She poured more coconut milk on the ends of the shaft to make sure the shaft would turn freely. Then she waited, listening to the rushing sounds of the water and the screeching of the birds.

Look at the picture of the water wheel.

Which part of the water wheel is A? Ⓢ

Which part is B? Ⓣ

What is C? Ⓤ

Touch A. Ⓥ Show which way A will move. Ⓦ

Touch the dot near B. Ⓧ Show which way the shaft will turn. Ⓨ

Touch the dot near C. Ⓩ Show which way that vine will move when the shaft turns. Ⓐ

 12 ERRORS

LESSON 73

1	2	3	4
beauty	burning	pressed	wrapped
orange	mosquito	unwound	kneeling
unpleasant	burst	squeaking	fire
jammed	brighter	wound	campfire
			decided

5	6	7
shell	drift	**Vocabulary words**
seashell	sunset	1. head of a nail
nails	drifts	2. thrash
fingernails	moment	3. raw
dunked	somewhere	4. dull
		5. glow
		6. imagine

B

A Rule about Things Rubbing Together

Today's story tells about things rubbing together. Here's the rule: **When things rub together, they get hotter.** Ⓐ

If you rub your hands together very fast, what will happen to your hands? Ⓑ

Rub them together and see if the rule works.©

What will happen if you rub two sticks together very fast?Ⓓ

The sticks may become hot enough to make a fire.

C The Water Wheel WorksⒶ

Linda was kneeling next to the water wheel.Ⓑ Linda waited for a long, long time. Suddenly, she felt a tug on the vine. She knew what that tug meant.© So she wrapped the end of the vine around the turning shaft. She was very careful not to get her hand too close to the shaft.Ⓓ The wheel was turning with great force.Ⓔ The vine started to move toward the shaft. It wrapped around the shaft.Ⓕ The shaft made a squeaking sound, and it seemed to bend a little bit. Faster and faster the vine wrapped around the shaft.   ❋ 2 ERRORS ❋

Linda couldn't see what was happening on the beach, but she imagined the net moving closer to the beach, filled with fish that were thrashing this way and that way.Ⓖ

After meters and meters of vine had
wrapped around the shaft, Linda stopped the
water wheel.Ⓗ Here's how she did that. She
took a heavy tree branch and jammed it under a
blade of the water wheel. The picture on the
next page shows the branch in place. The
blades couldn't turn, so the shaft couldn't
turn.Ⓘ

When the wheel stopped turning, Linda
followed the streambed down to the beach.
When she saw the net she stopped. It was about
ten meters from the ocean, and it was filled with
thrashing fish. ⓙ One fish looked bigger than
Kathy.

"Wow!" Linda said. "Do we ever have a lot
of fish to eat!"

"Let's put some of them back," Kathy said. "We can't eat all of these fish. Some of them are big enough for three meals." Ⓚ

So the girls put most of the fish back into the water. The fish swam far away from the rocks.

Kathy said, "We have fish now. But how are we going to cook them? I don't want to eat raw fish." Ⓛ

Linda said, "We'll have to think. There has to be some way to make a fire."

Kathy said, "What about rubbing two sticks together?" Ⓜ

Linda said, "I've tried that, and I could never get a fire."

Linda thought and thought. Finally she said, "I've got it!"

She ran over to the boards from the crate. She found a large nail. She walked back to the water wheel. She removed the vine and pounded the nail into one end of the shaft. Then she removed the large branch so the water wheel would turn. As the wheel turned, the head of the nail turned around and around. Ⓝ

Linda said, "I'm going to make that nail

red-hot. Help me find a nice big rock."

Kathy found a rock. Then Linda found some dry grass. She said, "As soon as that nail gets red-hot, hold some of the grass next to it. It will catch on fire. As soon as the grass starts to catch fire, put it on the ground."

Linda pressed the rock against the head of the nail. She pressed as hard as she could. The head of the nail kept turning. It rubbed against the rock. (P) "Sqrrrrr, sqrrrrr." (Q) Linda pressed harder and harder. The rock was rubbing against the head of the nail. The harder Linda pressed, the hotter the nail got.

"It's starting to turn red," Kathy said. (R)

At first the nail was dark gray. Then it became dull red. Then the red started to get brighter and brighter. Soon the nail was bright red. It was glowing. (S)

"Okay," Linda said. "Hold the grass next to the nail."

Kathy did, and the grass started to smoke. Then it burst into flames. (T) Kathy put the burning grass on the ground. Linda put some more grass on top of it. It started to burn. The fire was getting bigger. Kathy put some sticks on the grass. The sticks started to burn. The girls had made a fire. (U) ❁ 10 ERRORS ❁

LESSON 74

1
normal
fever
damage
sweat
comparison

2
beauty
mosquito
orange
fading

3
unhappy
somewhere
moment
drifts

4
knife
handle
dunked
buckle
fingernails

5
seashells
scrape
ugh
decided
campfire

6
built
wove
woven
more
anymore

7
mumble
chilled
head
forehead
mumbled

8
Vocabulary words
1. unpleasant
2. mumbled
3. few
4. sunset
5. foam
6. spray

B   The Girls Have Fish for Dinner Ⓐ

*The girls had made a fire by rubbing two objects together. Ⓑ One object had become red-hot from the rubbing. Ⓒ Now there was a nice warm campfire burning on the ground a few meters from the stream.

The girls had planned to cook fish up here by the waterfall, but the mosquitoes made the girls change their mind. Ⓓ As soon as the sun settled in the west and the jungle became dark, mosquitoes and other insects came out of the trees. Ⓔ

"Let's move our fire to the beach," Kathy said. Ⓕ

"Good idea," Linda said. 2 ERRORS

Each girl carried part of the* fire. Linda carried a coconut shell with a few burning sticks in it. Kathy carried a long stick that was burning on one end.

The girls decided to make a new fire on the rocks. The wind was strong out here and would drive the mosquitoes back into the jungle. Ⓖ The sisters built a very large fire on the rocks.

They then began the unpleasant task of cleaning the fish. Ⓗ "Ugh," Kathy said. "I don't want to do this."

"Me neither," Linda said. "But we've got to."

"I don't know how," Kathy said.

"We've got to scrape the scales off the outside of the fish. Then we have to take out the insides." Ⓘ

"Ugh," Kathy said. "I'll scrape the scales, but you'll have to do the insides."

"Okay," Linda said. Kathy used a seashell to scale the fish. She pressed a sharp end of the seashell against the fish and then scraped from

the tail of the fish toward the head.Ⓙ The scales popped off the fish. They were like little fingernails that you could see through.Ⓚ The scales stuck to everything. By the time Kathy had scaled two fish, her hair was covered with scales. So was her face. "Ugh," she said.Ⓛ

Linda made a knife from her belt buckle.Ⓜ She made the buckle sharp by rubbing it against a rock. She tied the buckle to a handle, which she made from a stick. She then used her knife to cut the fish open. She took out their insides and pulled out most of their bones.Ⓝ

•   •   •

There are very few places more beautiful than an island in the Pacific Ocean.Ⓞ And there are very few times of day more beautiful than sunset. The sun settles into the west, moving behind clouds that become filled with red and orange and yellow.Ⓟ The ocean looks dark, and the white foam and spray look gray in the fading light. The birds are quiet, and the breeze is sometimes warm and sometimes cool, as it gusts and stops and then gusts again.Ⓠ

That's how it was when Linda and Kathy ate their dinner that evening. They had some green plants that they had cooked with the fish. They boiled salt water to cook the plants in.Ⓡ They drank fresh water and ate the fish and plants.Ⓢ "This is about the most beautiful place in the world," Kathy said.

Linda nodded and looked out over the ocean toward the sunset. For a moment she felt the beauty of the sunset. Then she imagined that there were ships out there somewhere.Ⓣ Then she wondered how long it would be before one of those ships would find Kathy and her.Ⓤ Suddenly Linda felt cold and unhappy.Ⓥ

 9 ERRORS

LESSON 75

1	2	3	4
larva	S.S. Milton	woven	normal
surface	Captain Reeves	comparison	brain
rescue	S.S. Mason	tugboat	highest
cough	built	sliver	fever
survive	sweat		anymore

5	6	7
coughing	gather	paper
lower	survived	newspaper
damage	harbor	report
jungle	gathering	reporters
lowered		

8

Vocabulary words

1. chilled
2. forehead
3. rescued
4. moment
5. survived
6. mumbled

B Facts about Fevers

Your normal temperature is 37 degrees. That's the temperature inside your body when you are healthy.Ⓐ

Here are facts about fevers.Ⓑ

- When you have a fever, you are sick and your temperature goes up.Ⓒ
- Occasionally, a very sick person may have a fever of 42 degrees. This is about the highest fever someone can have.Ⓓ
- Most fevers don't go over 39 degrees.Ⓔ
- If a person has a very high fever for more than 12 hours, the fever may damage the person's brain.Ⓕ
- When people have high fevers, they may see things and hear things that are not happening.Ⓖ

C Signaling for Helpⓐ

By the time fourteen days had passed, Linda and Kathy were tired of fish and coconuts.Ⓑ They were waiting for a ship to come by. But no ship came. For two weeks, no ship came.Ⓒ

Then one day Linda and Kathy heard something. It was an airplane. They ran out onto the beach and looked into the sky. Where was it?Ⓓ

They looked and listened. It seemed as if they looked and listened for a long time. The sound of the plane got louder and louder, but still they couldn't see it. Then, all at once, it came over the trees.Ⓔ It was not very high. There it was, moving over the trees and over the beach. 🌸 2 ERRORS 🌸

The girls ran down the beach, waving their arms.Ⓕ They yelled, "Here we are. Here we are." They ran after the plane, but it went on, over the ocean.Ⓖ "Here we are. Here we are," they called.

They watched the plane get smaller and smaller and smaller. "Come back. Come back!" Kathy yelled. The girls watched it until they couldn't see it anymore.Ⓗ

"Maybe it will come back," Kathy said.

The girls looked at the sky for at least an hour.Ⓘ Then Kathy started to cry. "We'll never get off this island."

"Don't talk like that," Linda said. "We will get off this island. That plane didn't see us because we didn't give the plane much to see. So we'll make things that any plane or ship will see. Ⓙ We'll start right now by getting some rocks—lots of them."

The girls carried rock after rock onto the beach and put each rock in place. Soon the rocks formed the letters H and E. Ⓚ Each letter was over two meters high. The girls got more rocks. Now the rocks formed H-E-L. They got more rocks. Now the rocks formed H-E-L-P. Ⓛ The word was over fifteen meters long. Ⓜ

When they had finished, Kathy said, "A plane should be able to see that."

Linda said, "Right, but a ship won't. Ⓝ We have to make another signal for ships."

The girls went to the highest hill in the jungle. They built a fire on the hill. Then they went back into the jungle to get lots and lots of green leaves. Ⓞ

Linda said, "We'll keep a big pile of leaves next to the fire. We'll keep the fire going all the time. When we see a ship, we'll dump the green leaves on the fire. Ⓟ The leaves will make a lot of smoke."

The girls kept the fire going for four days. On the fourth day, Kathy had a fever. Ⓠ Linda felt Kathy's forehead. It felt much hotter than a normal temperature. Ⓡ In fact, Linda thought that Kathy's temperature was over 39 degrees. Ⓢ

During the day Kathy slept on the hill near the fire. Occasionally, she woke up. Ⓣ Once, she mumbled something in her sleep about "the ship, the ship." The girls had woven some mats from leaves and vines. When the sun began to set in the west, Linda covered Kathy with one of these mats.Ⓤ She did that so Kathy wouldn't become too chilled by the cool air.Ⓥ

Just as the sky was turning bright yellow and orange, Kathy sat up. "A ship," she said. Her eyes were wide. She pointed to the south. "A ship. I see a ship."Ⓦ

"Take it easy," Linda said, putting her hands on Kathy's shoulders.Ⓧ

"No, no," Kathy shouted. "There's a ship." Her body was shaking. 🌸 10 ERRORS 🌸

LESSON 76

A

1	2	3	4
terrible	Captain Reeves	surface	sliver
attack	S.S. Mason	harbor	lowered
behave	S.S. Milton	tugboat	gather
serious	bead	sweat	sight
	larva	crowded	

5	6
scar	**Vocabulary words**
excited	**1.** newspaper reporter
comparison	**2.** cough
scarred	**3.** rescued
single	**4.** moment
	5. survive

B

Landing a Ship

Landing a ship is a lot like landing an airplane. Here is a comparison: Ⓐ

- Airplanes land in airports. Ships land in harbors. Ⓑ
- Airplanes load and unload at gates. Ships load and unload at docks. Ⓒ

- Sometimes a little truck pulls an airplane to the gate. Sometimes a little boat pulls a large ship to the dock.

The boat that pulls the ships is called a tugboat. **(D)** The picture shows a tugboat pulling the S.S. Milton into a busy harbor in Japan. **(E)** Along the shore are many docks with ships parked at them. **(F)**

C

The Girls Are Rescued Ⓐ

Linda didn't really believe that there was a ship in sight. Ⓑ But Linda slowly turned her head and looked south. She saw dark water and more dark water and a shiny sliver of white. Ⓒ It was a ship—a ship with the sun shining on one side of it. Ⓓ "A ship," Linda said out loud.

Kathy raised her arms and waved. "Hello," she hollered. Ⓔ

"They must be three kilometers away," Linda said. "They won't be able to hear us. We've got to make a smoke signal." Ⓕ

The girls dumped all the green leaves on the fire. For a few moments it seemed that the fire was going out. Then large billows of smoke rolled into the air. Ⓖ ❉ 2 ERRORS ❉

The shiny sliver on the ocean seemed to be getting larger. Ⓗ "More smoke," Kathy hollered. The girls threw heaps of grass on the fire. The fire coughed out bigger and bigger billows. Ⓘ

The ship was an ocean liner like the one that Linda and Kathy had been on. Now Linda could see people standing on the deck.

"It's stopping!" Kathy yelled. "The ship is stopping!" Linda and her sister ran down the hill. Linda fell and cut her leg. But she didn't notice it. Ⓙ Linda got up and ran as fast as she could until she reached the shore. She waved her arms.

A little boat was slowly lowered down the side of the great ocean liner. The little boat started toward the shore. Ⓚ Linda was crying for the first time since the ship went down three weeks before. Ⓛ "We're going home," Linda said. "We're going home."

The boat came up to the beach. The girls ran into the ocean to meet the boat. One of the three men in the boat said, "I'm Captain Reeves from the ship S.S. Milton." Ⓜ

Linda said, "I'm Linda Jones and this is my sister, Kathy. We were on the ship S.S. Mason when it sank."

Linda looked at Kathy and smiled. Then she remembered that Kathy was sick. "Kathy's sick," Linda said.

The captain felt Kathy's forehead and ordered the men in the boat to take her to the ship. Linda and the captain stayed on the island so that Linda could show how she and her sister survived for three weeks. **(N)**

It was getting fairly dark by the time they reached the water wheel. **(O)** "Amazing," the captain said. Linda showed the knife she made and the signal for airplanes that was on the beach. "Amazing," the captain said again. **(P)** "You're a very smart girl."

Linda felt very proud and very excited. The excitement seemed to continue all the way to

Japan. Linda and her sister were stars on the S.S. Milton.Ⓠ Everybody wanted to talk to them and ask them questions or go swimming with them. The girls ate at the captain's table. Only very important people eat at the captain's table.Ⓡ

Kathy felt better the day after the girls left the island. The girls were on the S.S. Milton for one week.Ⓢ When a tugboat finally pulled the ship into the harbor at Japan, horns tooted and many small boats crowded around the S.S. Milton.Ⓣ The girls' father met them at the dock. There were newspaper reporters in the crowd, too.Ⓤ The reporters asked the girls many questions.

Then their father drove them to their new house in Japan. It was a very pretty house on a small hill with a large tree in the front yard. Linda's father said, "You've done so many things lately that you may find it dull living here."Ⓥ

Linda hugged her father. "No, daddy, it won't be dull," she said. "I'm just glad to be here."

Kathy said, "Me, too." ❀ 10 ERRORS ❀

LESSON 77

A

1	2	3	4
involve	single	batter	**Vocabulary**
constantly	scarred	surface	**words**
among	terrible	battered	1. scar
describe	involved	larva	2. attack
calm			3. behave
perhaps			4. reply

B

Facts about Mosquitoes

Here are some facts about mosquitoes: Ⓐ

- Mosquitoes are insects. Ⓑ
- Mosquitoes are born from eggs. Ⓒ
- Mosquitoes are born in water. Ⓓ
- When the mosquito lives in the water, it doesn't look like a mosquito. It is called a **larva.** The larva hangs down from the skin at the surface of the water. So the water must be very still. Ⓔ

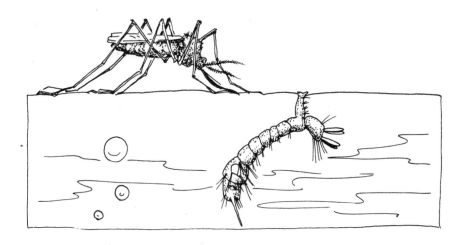

- After a few days, the larva turns into a mosquito.Ⓕ
- Only female mosquitoes bite.Ⓖ

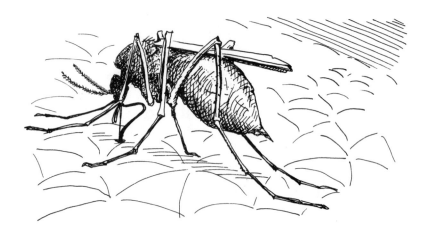

- When mosquitoes bite, they suck blood.
- They cannot lay eggs until they suck blood.Ⓗ

C The Scarred Words in the Word Bank Ⓐ

If you look at the words in the word bank, you'll notice that some of them have scars. These scars came from great fights that used to take place right in the word bank. The words no longer fight, but thousands of years ago when Hohoboho was a very young country, there were hundreds of terrible fights. Ⓑ Words would leap out of their seats and attack other words. They would hit and fight and scratch and yell and throw things and behave like a bunch of animals. From these fights some words got their scars. ✿ 2 ERRORS ✿

Not all the words have scars. The word **wash** does not have one single scar. Neither does the word **only** or the word **run.** But the word **red** has scars. The word **their** is covered with scars. So is the word **two.**

Here's the story about why some words are scarred: When the word bank opened for the first time, the words were given their seats. The people in Hohoboho would talk, and every time one of the words was said, that word would get one point. But there was a very bad problem. Some words sounded just like other words. When somebody in Hohoboho said, "It is over **there**," the word **there** would say, "That's me. I get that point." The word **their** would say, "No, that's me. The person said **their**."

"Wrong," the word **there** would reply. "Any fool could hear them say **there**." Ⓒ

By now both words would be standing up and hollering at each other. "Who are you calling a fool?" the word **their** would be shouting.

"You, you fool," the word **there** would reply. And the words would start swinging and scratching and throwing things. Ⓓ

The fight would continue until the words were tired out. Ⓔ By then somebody in Hohoboho would say something like, "Do they have a radio in **their** car?"

The word **their** would jump up, "That's me." Ⓕ

"No way," the word **there** would reply. "Somebody said **there** and that's me."

Soon, they would be fighting again.

As **their** and **there** fought, somebody in Hohoboho would say, "Speak louder. I can't **hear** you." **G** The word **hear** would jump up and say, "That's me." Another word would also jump up and say, "No, that's me." Then **here** and **hear** would get into a terrible fight. **H**

In other parts of the word bank, other words would be shouting and fighting. **I**

LESSON 78

A

1	2	3
among	eight	**Vocabulary words**
perhaps	plugs	1. involved
calm	earplugs	2. constantly
describe	screen	3. battered
		4. worst

B

Henry Ouch Takes a Vacation

Henry Ouch went for a vacation. **Ⓐ** He left San Francisco on a large ship. That ship went to Japan. You know which direction it went. **Ⓑ**

How far was that trip? **Ⓒ**

What ocean did Henry cross? **Ⓓ**

The ship passed some islands. How did Henry know they were islands? **Ⓔ** Henry could see palm trees on some islands. He knew the name for branches of a palm tree. **Ⓕ** He also knew the name of the large hard things that grow on some palm trees. **Ⓖ** When Henry got thirsty, he drank little drops of water that formed on the deck early in the morning. What are those drops called?Ⓗ

Henry did not drink water from the ocean. Why not?Ⓘ

Henry was very strong, but he could not carry a liter of fresh water. How heavy is a liter of fresh water?Ⓙ

Henry did not like it when the temperature dropped down because Henry's body worked like the bodies of other insects. Henry was _____-blooded.Ⓚ Sometimes the temperature inside his body was higher than your normal temperature.Ⓛ

Sometimes the temperature inside his body was lower than your normal temperature.Ⓜ

C The Number with the Most ScarsⒶ

The words in the word bank had a problem because they listened to the words that were said by the people in Hohoboho.Ⓑ Some words sound the same. When the people in Hohoboho said these words, the words that sounded the same would fight over who got the point. The words **their** and **there** were always fighting. But they were not the only ones. Ⓒ The words for numbers were involved in some of the worst fights you could imagine. Ⓓ The word **three** never fought. Ⓔ Nor did the words **five, six,** or **seven.** But **one, two, four,** and **eight** went from one fight to another. ✿ 2 ERRORS ✿

The word **one** fought with the word **won.** Ⓕ Every time somebody in Hohoboho said, ''I **won,**'' a fight would take place. Every time somebody in Hohoboho said, ''You have **one** more turn,'' another fight would take place. Ⓖ

The word **four** was always fighting with **for.** If somebody in Hohoboho said, ''I will do something **for** you,'' the words **for** and **four** would fight. They also fought when somebody said, ''I have **four** spoons.''

The word **eight** was always fighting with the word **ate.** If somebody said, ''A man **ate** an egg,'' there would be a fight. The word **eight** would say, ''That's me. He said **eight.**'' The word **ate** would say, ''You're crazy. He said **ate.**'' And the fight would start.

Eight, four, and **one** had terrible fights and

lots of them, but their fights could not compare to the fights that the word **two** used to have. **H** If you look at **two** now, you can get some idea of how bad those fights were. **I** **Two** has scars and scars and scars. The reason is that **two** used to fight constantly. **J** **Two** used to fight with the word **to**. Every time somebody would say, "Go **to** the store," **two** would say, "That's me. She said **two**." Soon, **two** and **to** would be fighting.

But **two** also had fights with **too.** If somebody said, "I'll go, **too,**" **two** would say, "Another point for me. She said **two.**" "No," **too** would say. "She said **too.**" By now the word **to** would say, "You're both crazy," and a *big* fight would start.(K)

By the end of the day, when the people in Hohoboho stopped talking and went to bed, some of the words in the word bank were pretty battered up.(L) The word **two** was always among the words that were most battered. **Two** was usually glad when the day was over. **Two** needed the rest before starting another day of battles with **too** and **to.** 🌀 6 ERRORS 🌀

LESSON 79

A

1	2
screen	**Vocabulary words**
spelling	**1.** describe
noisy	**2.** calm
rhyme	**3.** earplugs
claim	**4.** perhaps
difference	

B

A Pilot's Trip

A jet pilot went around the world. She went from the country of Japan to Italy. In what direction was she going?Ⓐ

Then she continued in the same·direction until she came to a country that is much larger than Japan or Italy.Ⓑ She landed her jet plane in a city on the east coast of the country.Ⓒ

When the wheels of the plane touched the runway, they rubbed against the runway and you know what happened to the temperature of the wheels.Ⓓ

The pilot was not feeling well. She thought she had a slight fever.Ⓔ So she went to a doctor. The doctor told her that her temperature was normal.Ⓕ The doctor said, "You need more exercise. You should walk at least one thousand meters every day." The pilot knew another name for **a thousand meters.**Ⓖ

The pilot took off and flew to Japan. She left her plane and took a vacation. She went to a place where there was a water wheel. Every second, one liter of water hit the blades of that wheel. You know how much weight that is.Ⓗ Around the water were insects that were born in the water and sucked blood. You know what they were.Ⓘ

The pilot stayed away from these insects.Ⓙ She had a nice vacation.

C   Some Words Stop FightingⒶ

The word bank was a mess. That's the best way to describe it.Ⓑ Early in the morning, before the people in Hohoboho started to talk, things in the word bank would be calm.Ⓒ But before long a fight would start. Somebody in

Hohoboho would say, "I have **new** shoes," and the fight would start between **new** and **knew.** Ⓓ

Then the people in Hohoboho would start talking more and more and more. And fights would start all over the word bank. It would become so noisy that some of the words wore earplugs.Ⓔ When a word wore earplugs it could not hear if it was said, but the words in the back of the bank didn't care.Ⓕ 🌀 2 ERRORS 🌀

The word **billows** almost always wore earplugs. The word **usually** sat near **billows.**

Once **usually** pulled an earplug from **billows's**
ear and asked, "Why do you wear earplugs?
Don't you want to hear your name said?"

"Sure," **billows** replied. "But I'm not going
to be said more than once or twice a day, and I'd
rather have it quiet than listen to all this
fighting and shouting." **G**

*After a while, things got so bad in the
word bank that a change was made. **H** If that
change hadn't been made, some of the words
might have been battered to pieces in the
terrible fights they had. But one morning there
was an announcement. A voice came over the
loud-speaker and said, "From now on, the
words will appear on the screen when the
people in Hohoboho say them. You will not hear
what the people say. But you will see how the
words are spelled. If a word is spelled the same
way as a word on the* screen, that word gets a
point." **I**

The words looked at each other. The word
their looked at **there.** The word **their** said, "I
think that will work. My spelling is different
from your spelling. If they write the words, we
will be able to tell if the word is **their** or **there.**"

And that's just what happened. When the words were said by the people in Hohoboho, the words would appear on a large screen. And that was the very last fight that **two** had or that **there** had or that **eight** had. The word **one** shook hands with the word **won.** "This is great," the word **one** said. The word **hear** and the word **here** also shook hands. Ⓙ

. There wasn't any word happier about this change than the word **two.** Ⓚ For the first time since the word bank opened, the word **two** could jump up and say, "That's me. They said **two,**" without getting into a fight with **to** and **too.**

The change in the word bank stopped the fights among words that sound the same. But there was a new problem. As soon as the words appeared on the screen, fights started among words that had never fought before. Can you think of why these fights would take place? Ⓛ

 7 ERRORS

LESSON 80

A

1	2	3	4
contraction	difference	whisper	**Vocabulary**
electric	finger	aren't	**words**
war	rhyme	she'd	claim
soldier	smoothly	whispered	
sword			

B

Another Announcement Is Made Ⓐ

New fights started in the word bank as soon as the words were written on the screen. To understand the problem that took place in the word bank, you have to understand that some words are spelled the same way but are not said the same way. They sound different. Ⓑ

Two words are spelled with the letters **r-o-w.** One of those words rhymes with **now.** Say that word. Ⓒ The other word that is spelled **r-o-w** rhymes with **go.** Say that word. Ⓓ

The two words that are spelled **r-o-w** never fought until the words were written on the screen. But as soon as the words appeared on the screen, these words fought. 🌸 2 ERRORS 🌸

When somebody in Hohoboho would say, "Let's plant these seeds in a **row,**" the two words spelled **r-o-w** would jump up. "That's me," they would start yelling. Soon they would be fighting. Ⓔ

Two other words that are spelled the same are spelled **w-i-n-d.** One of those words rhymes with **find.** Ⓕ The other word rhymes with **pinned.** Ⓖ But every time the word spelled **w-i-n-d** appeared on the screen, these two words started to fight over who got the point. Ⓗ

Some terrible fights took place over the word spelled **r-e-a-d.** Ⓘ Somebody in Hohoboho would say, "Did you **read** that?" The other person would answer, "Yes, I **read** that." Both words spelled **r-e-a-d** would get into a terrible row.

Another pair of words that had some bad fights are spelled **t-e-a-r.** Ⓙ Somebody in Hohoboho would say, "I think you're crying. Is that a **tear** in your eye?" And both words would try to claim the point. Ⓚ "That's me," they would shout. The same words would fight when somebody said, "Take that paper and **tear** it up."

If you looked at the words that were involved in these fights, you'd see that they have some small scars, but not many scars and not very bad ones. Ⓛ Compared to the word **two,** the words spelled **t-e-a-r** would look as if they had never been in a fight. Ⓜ Here's the reason that the words with the same spelling are not very scarred: A few days after the fights started another announcement was made. The voice said, "From now on, the words will go on the screen. Then a voice will read the words. Ⓝ Here's how a word in the word bank gets a point. That word must be spelled the same as the word on the screen. The word must also sound the same as the word the voice reads." Ⓞ

The word **slow** said, "I don't understand that rule."

The word **smart** said, "It's easy. If you're spelled like the word on the screen and if you sound like that word, you get the point."

The word **confusion** said, "It sounds too hard."

The word **clear** said, "Look at it this way. If

you get mixed up, I'll tell you if you get the point.''

Lazy said, ''That sounds good to me.''

Then the words with problems began to talk. ⓟ

One of the words spelled **t-e-a-r** said, ''That makes sense. If somebody says my name, we will hear it. We don't have to fight.'' ⓠ

The words spelled **r-e-a-d** agreed. ⓡ ''You can hear the difference when somebody says, 'I will **read** a book' or says 'Yesterday, I **read** a book.' ''

So there was a big change in the word bank. The words that sound like other words would look at the screen to see which word was said. The word **two** didn't fight with the words that sounded the same.Ⓢ And the words that are spelled the same never had a problem because they listened to the voice. If the voice said, "That is a **live** fish," the sound of the word would tell who got the point.Ⓣ Most of the problems in the word bank were solved.

 8 ERRORS

LESSON 81

A

1	2	3
shield	contractions	soldiers
weapon	she'd	wars
protect	aren't	ago
calendar	electric	starve
	swords	Troy

4

Vocabulary words

1. smooth and quiet
2. whisper

B   CONTRACTIONS

Contractions are words made by joining two words together. Ⓐ Part of one word is missing. This mark ' is used to show where the part is missing. Ⓑ

Here are some contractions and the words that make them up:

- **couldn't** is made up of **could** and **not** Ⓒ
- **he'll** is made up of **he** and **will** Ⓓ

- **you've** is made up of **you** and **have** Ⓔ

Say the words that make up each contraction below. Ⓕ

a. we've is made up of ＿＿ and ＿＿ Ⓖ

b. you're is made up of ＿＿ and ＿＿ Ⓗ

c. can't is made up of ＿＿ and ＿＿ Ⓘ

d. I'll is made up of ＿＿ and ＿＿ Ⓙ

C

The Last Problem in the Word Bank Is Solved Ⓐ

Perhaps you think that all the problems in the word bank had been solved. The words that sound the same as other words were no longer fighting. Ⓑ The words that are spelled the same as other words were friends again. Ⓒ Almost everything was going smoothly. There was still one problem, however. Words that are contractions had fights. Here are some contractions: **you're, I'll, can't, couldn't, shouldn't, aren't, she'd.** Can you name some other contractions? Ⓓ

The contractions fought because contractions are made up of two words. The contraction **couldn't** is made up of the words **could** and **not**. ❋ 2 ERRORS ❋

The contraction **you're** is made up of the words **you** and **are.** The contraction **I'll** is made up of the words **I** and **will.** What words make up the contraction **shouldn't?**Ⓔ

When contractions are formed, part of one of the words is left out. The left-out part is marked with this mark: '. In the word **couldn't,** the mark shows that the letter **o** is missing. In the word **you'll,** the mark shows that the letters **w** and **i** are missing. In the word **you've,** the mark shows that the letters **h** and **a** are missing. What letters are missing in the contraction **we've?**Ⓕ

Here's what used to happen in the word bank. Whenever a contraction was named, the two words that make up the contraction would fight. For example, when the contraction **you'll** was said, the word **you** would say, ''That's me.'' The word **will** would say, ''No, that's me.'' A third word would join the fight. That word was the contraction **you'll.** So a big row would go on between **you'll, you,** and **will.**

Which three words would fight when

someone in Hohoboho said **he'll?**Ⓖ Which three words would fight when someone said **shouldn't?**Ⓗ

By now, the other words in the word bank were tired of seeing words fight. "Come on," the word **calm** said. "Why don't you figure out some way of solving the problem? Do you have to wait for another announcement?"

"Yeah," the word **smart** said. "We can work out a plan that will make everybody happy."

The word **question** asked, "What kind of plan would that be?"

So the word **smart** thought for a moment and then came up with this plan: every time a contraction is said, three words get points. The contraction that is said gets one point. ⓘ The word in the contraction that has all its letters gets one point. ⓙ The word in the contraction that has some letters missing does not get one point. That word gets half a point. Ⓚ **Smart** said, "Remember, the contraction and the full word each get one point." Ⓛ

The contraction **shouldn't** said, "I think I understand. If somebody says **shouldn't,** I get one point. And **should** gets one point because it has all its letters."

The word **not** said, "And I only get half a point because one of my letters is missing in the word **shouldn't.**" Ⓜ

The plan worked, and the fighting finally ended in the word bank. When a word like **you'll** is said, the contraction **you'll** gets one point. The word **you** gets one point because it has no part missing. The word **will** gets half a point because it has a part missing. **(N)**

"Things are very nice in the word bank now," the word **calm** said when the plan was first used.

"Yes, things are nice," the word **quiet** whispered. ✿ 10 ERRORS ✿

LESSON 82

A

1	2	3
Jesus Christ	weapons	protect
Greece	ladders	electric
suppose	queen	tanks
succeed	starve	Helen
secret	ago	calendar

4	5
swords	spears
dump	army
shields	battle
Troy	war
soldier	

B

Greece and Sparta

The next story that you will read tells about a war between Troy and Greece. Ⓐ You can find Troy and Greece on the map of the world. The place that was called Troy is now part of Turkey. Ⓑ The place called Greece is between

Italy and Turkey. Italy is shaped like a boot, and it looks like it is ready to step on Greece. ©

The map below makes it easier to see Troy and Greece. The war took place at Troy. The story that you'll read tells why that war took place. Ⓓ

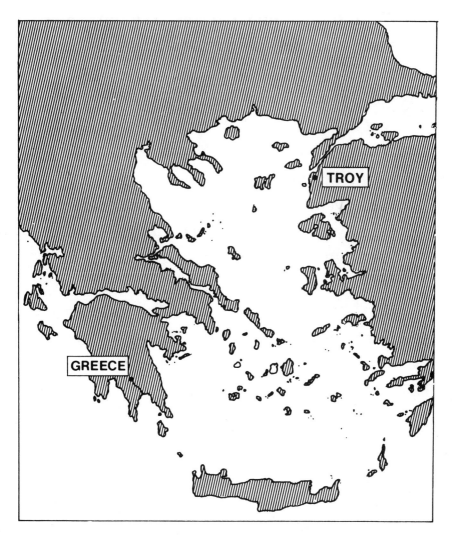

C LEARNING ABOUT A TIME LINE

You're going to read a story about something that took place a long time ago. To understand how long ago the story happened, you have to understand how a calendar works. Ⓐ

If the year is now 1990, the year 1 hundred years ago was 1890. If the year is now 1985, the year 1 hundred years ago was 1885.

What year is it really now? Ⓑ

What year was it 1 hundred years ago? Ⓒ

What year were you born? Ⓓ

What year was it 1 hundred years before the time you were born? Ⓔ

Here's a rule about years. **The numbers get smaller as you go back in time.** Ⓕ ❋ 2 ERRORS ❋

What are the first two numbers in the year 1970? Ⓖ

If you go back 1 hundred years, the first two numbers would be 18. So the year 1 hundred years before 1970 is 1870. Ⓗ

What are the first two numbers in the year 1679? Ⓘ If you go back 1 hundred years, the first two numbers wouldn't be 16. They would be 15. So what year is 1 hundred years before 1679? Ⓙ

What are the first two numbers in the year 1965? Ⓚ If you go back 1 hundred years, what are the first two numbers? Ⓛ If you go back another 1 hundred years, what are the first two numbers? Ⓜ If you go back another 1 hundred years, what are the first two numbers? Ⓝ

What year is 3 hundred years before 1965? Ⓞ

Start with the year 1780. If you went back 2 hundred years, what are the first numbers? Ⓟ Say the year that is 2 hundred years before 1780. Ⓠ

The arrow in the picture on page 73 shows a time line. Here's the rule about the time line: **Things that happen right now are at the top of the time line.** Ⓡ

Things that happened a long time ago are near the bottom of the time line. Ⓢ

Touch the dot that says **now**. Ⓣ What year should go on that dot? Ⓤ Now touch dot B. Ⓥ That dot shows when you were born. That dot is very close to the top dot because you were born only a few years ago. What year goes on dot B?Ⓦ

Now touch dot C.Ⓧ That dot shows that the first airplane was made around 1900. That was almost 1 hundred years ago.

Touch dot D.Ⓨ That dot shows the year 1 hundred years ago. What year was that?Ⓩ

Touch dot E.Ⓐ That dot shows the year 2 hundred years ago. What year was that?Ⓑ

Dot F shows the year that the United States became a country. What year was that?Ⓒ

Touch dot G.Ⓓ That dot shows the year 3 hundred years ago. What year was that?Ⓔ

See how many of the dates you can remember without looking at the time line. What year is it now?Ⓕ

What year were you born?Ⓖ

Around what year was the first airplane made?Ⓗ

What was the year 1 hundred years ago?Ⓘ

What was the year 2 hundred years ago?Ⓙ

In what year did the United States become a country?Ⓚ

What was the year 3 hundred years ago?Ⓛ

 7 ERRORS

A • now

B • You were born.

C • 1900: The first airplane was made.

D • 1 hundred years ago

E • 2 hundred years ago

F • 1776: The United States became
  a country.

G • 3 hundred years ago

LESSON 83

1	2	3
swords	spears	**Vocabulary words**
electric	Troy	**1.** war
weapons	shields	**2.** battle
dump	Helen	**3.** army
tanks	queen	**4.** soldier
	ladders	**5.** protect
		6. starve

B

The City of Troy Ⓐ

The story that you're going to read about took place a long time ago. It didn't take place one hundred years ago or two hundred years ago or three hundred years ago. It took place about 3 thousand years ago. Ⓑ It took place long before airplanes or cars were made. It took place long before the United States became a country. Ⓒ

The story took place 3 thousand years ago in a city called Troy. Ⓓ The map shows that Herman flew right over Troy and Greece on his way to Italy. Ⓔ Troy was in the country that is now Turkey. ✿ 2 ERRORS ✿

Troy was different from any city you have ever seen because there were no cars or buses in Troy.(F) There were no telephones or televisions. There were no electric lights or refrigerators. The people in Troy had never seen any of these things because these things had not been made yet. There were no street lights or trains. There were no planes and no guns. Although the people who lived in Troy did not have guns, they had battles and wars. They used bows and arrows and spears in these wars.(G)

The city of Troy had a great wall around it. The wall was so high that you could not jump over it and you could not climb over it unless you had a very tall ladder. When the people inside Troy went in and out of the city, they went through a great gate that was as tall as the wall.(H) When the people inside Troy did not want someone to come inside the city, they closed the great gate. This gate was so strong that an elephant could not knock it down. In fact, it was so strong that ten elephants could not knock it down. Here's the rule about Troy: When the gate was closed, you could not get into the city.(I)

Sometimes Troy went to war with another city. An army would come to Troy. This army did not have jets and tanks. ⓙ This army did not have cars and great guns. But this army had soldiers—lots of soldiers. And the soldiers had horses and ladders. The soldiers had shovels. The soldiers had swords and shields.

The picture shows some of the weapons the soldiers had.

The soldier is holding a sword in one hand.Ⓚ The soldier is holding a shield with the other hand. The shield is used to protect the soldier against swords and spears.Ⓛ

A spear is standing next to the soldier. You use a spear by throwing it.Ⓜ

A bow and some arrows are lying on the ground.Ⓝ

In back of the soldier are a ladder and a shovel.Ⓞ That ladder is used to help the soldier climb high walls. The shovel helps the soldier dig under walls.

The army would try to get inside the city by using these plans:

1. The army would try to get over the wall.Ⓟ

2. The army would try to dig under the wall.Ⓠ

3. The army would try to knock down the gate using great tree trunks on wheels.

4. The army would not let anybody out of the city so that the people inside would get very hungry.

For every plan that the army had, the people in Troy had a plan.Ⓡ

1. When the army would put ladders against the wall, the people of Troy would push the ladders over.Ⓢ

2. When the army would dig holes under the wall, the people of Troy would dump boiling water into the holes.Ⓣ

3. When the army would try to knock

down the gate, the people of Troy would shoot the soldiers with arrows and dump boiling water on them. Ⓤ

4. The army could not starve the people of Troy because the people of Troy had lots of food and water inside the wall.

In the next story, you will read about a great war that took place in Troy. This war lasted a long, long time because the army could not get inside the wall. ❋ 10 ERRORS ❋

LESSON 84

A

1	2	3	4
Jesus Christ	hammer	saw	**Vocabulary**
Greece	Helen	quiet	**words**
queen	hammered	quietly	**1.** succeeded
Greek	supposed	sawed	**2.** secret

When the Story of Troy Took Place

Time line A shows how long ago the story of Troy took place. You know how the time line works. Which things are at the top of the time line?Ⓐ Which things are near the bottom of the time line?Ⓑ

Touch dot A.Ⓒ That's the year now. What year is that?Ⓓ

Touch dot B.Ⓔ That's the year 1 hundred years ago. What year was that?Ⓕ

Touch dot C.Ⓖ That's the year 2 hundred years ago. What year was that?Ⓗ

Touch the dot that shows 1 thousand years ago.Ⓘ

Touch the dot that shows 2 thousand years ago.Ⓙ That was around the time that Jesus Christ was alive.

We have to go back 1 thousand more years before we reach the time that the story of Troy took place.

Touch dot F.Ⓚ What time does that dot show?Ⓛ

What happened 3 thousand years ago?Ⓜ

Time Line A

A   now
B   1 hundred years ago
C   2 hundred years ago

D   1 thousand years ago

E   2 thousand years ago

F   3 thousand years ago

Look at time line B. It has the same dots as the other time line. See if you can touch the right dot for each time.

Touch the dot that shows 2 thousand years ago. Ⓝ

Touch the dot that shows 2 hundred years ago. Ⓞ

Touch the dot that shows 3 thousand years ago. Ⓟ

Touch the dot that shows 1 hundred years ago. Ⓠ

About how long ago did Jesus Christ live? Ⓡ

How long ago did the story of Troy take place? Ⓢ

Time Line B

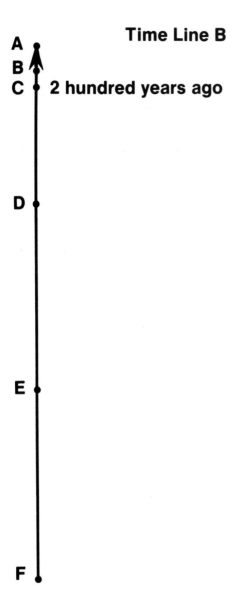

A

B

C 2 hundred years ago

D

E

F

C A Great War at Troy Ⓐ

There are stories about a great war that took place at Troy. Some of the stories are make-believe and some are real.

These stories say that the war took place because a man from Troy fell in love with a woman from Greece. The man from Troy was the son of the king. The woman from Greece was named Helen. Ⓑ She was supposed to be the most beautiful woman in the world. And she was a queen of a city in Greece. Ⓒ When Helen fell in love, she left her city and went to Troy. The people of her city wanted their queen back, but she wouldn't come back. Ⓓ   ❀ 2 ERRORS ❀

So part of Greece went to war with Troy. To reach Troy, the soldiers had to cross part of an ocean. A thousand ships sailed to Troy. The army that sailed in those ships was the largest army ever seen. Ⓔ When the ships reached Troy, the army poured from the ships—soldiers, horses, shields, swords, shovels, and food. Ⓕ The army set up camp outside the great wall of Troy. Ⓖ There were men and tents from the wall

all the way to the sea. And along the shore of the sea were ships and ships and more ships. Ⓗ

*Now the battle began. Soldiers from Greece rode on horses around the great wall. Soldiers of Troy shot at them with bows and arrows. Soldiers from Greece rushed to the wall with ladders and tried to climb over the wall. They did not succeed. Ⓘ

The army tried to dig under the wall. Men dug and dug, but they did not succeed. Ⓙ

The army cut down great tree trunks and put wheels on them. Soldiers pushed the tree trunks toward the gate, but they did not knock the gate down. Ⓚ

The army tried to starve the people inside Troy, but that* didn't work either. Ⓛ

The war went on for month after month and year after year. The same things happened day after day. The army tried to get inside the city, but the people of Troy kept the army out.

The war went on for ten years. Ⓜ For ten years, the army of Greece failed. The men in that army got older and tired of the war. They said, "If only we could get a few men inside the wall, they could open the huge gates and let the rest of the army inside." Ⓝ

That was the secret. Four men inside the wall could open the gate. Three men inside the wall could open the gate. But for ten years, the army of Greece was not able to get one soldier inside the wall. ❋ 6 ERRORS ❋

LESSON 85

A

1	2	3	4
student	peanuts	quietly	Bertha
donkey	however	Greeks	track
directly	blindfold	sawed	trackers
talent	playground	post	sailed
		hammered	

5	6	7
blink	study	**Vocabulary words**
amaze	lazy	**1.** failed
amazement	lazier	**2.** gift
lemon	normal	**3.** sense
blinked	normally	**4.** peek

B

The Great Wooden Horse Ⓐ

For ten years, the army of Greece tried to get inside the wall of Troy, but for ten years the soldiers failed. The army kept using the same four plans over and over, but the plans failed again and again. Ⓑ But the army kept on trying to get a few men inside the wall.

During the tenth year of the war somebody had an idea for a new plan. The army started to work on this plan. Soldiers cut down great trees. Soldiers hammered and sawed wood. They were making something from wood. But what was it? ✿ 2 ERRORS ✿

The people inside Troy watched from the wall. As the days went by, they saw what it was. It was a great horse—a great wooden horse. And it was huge. It stood very tall, and it had wooden wheels.

"What are they going to do?" the people in Troy asked each other.

One night the soldiers of Greece rolled the huge wooden horse in front of the gate. Then the soldiers left. They got in the ships, and the ships sailed from the shore.

"The war must be over," the people of Troy said.©

The people of Troy looked outside, but they could see no Greek soldiers. There were no tents, no ships, and no horses. Everything was quiet.

"Maybe the horse is a gift," they said to each other. "Maybe the Greeks left this gift to tell us that we won the war."Ⓓ

Slowly, the soldiers of Troy went outside the gate. They looked all around the city to see if the Greek army was trying to trick them, but no Greeks could be seen.

Suddenly, the people of Troy began to cheer and shout.Ⓔ For ten years they had been at war. "The war is over," they shouted. "We have won the war."

The huge gates opened wide, and the people of Troy rolled the huge wooden horse inside. When the horse was inside, the people closed the gate. Then they yelled, "Let's have a party." So they did. They ate and laughed and sang songs and danced until late at night. Then they went to sleep, very happy. Ⓕ

That is when something very strange happened. Part of the great horse started to move. That part was a door. Slowly the door on the horse opened. One man came out of the door. Then another man came out of the door. These men were soldiers from Greece. The horse was not a gift. It was a trick. And the trick had worked. Ⓖ

The ships had not gone back to Greece. They had sailed until they could not be seen by the people of Troy. They waited until the sun went down. While the people of Troy were dancing and singing, the ships sailed back to the shore. And when the people of Troy went to sleep very happy, the soldiers from Greece moved quietly toward the great gate. For ten years, they had tried to get a few men inside the wall, and now they had done it. Ⓗ

The men who had been inside the horse slid down a rope. They ran to the huge gate. Slowly, the gate opened. Ⓘ

Now, the people of Troy were starting to wake up. But it was too late. Hundreds and hundreds of soldiers from Greece came through the gate. Before the soldiers of Troy could get their swords and spears, the war was over. The army of Greece had won.

The story of the wooden horse may be make-believe. But we know that there was a great war between Greece and Troy. And the story of Troy tells us something that is important. If you can't solve a problem one way, try something else.

The army of Greece kept trying to get inside the walls by using their old tricks. Then they tried something else. It worked. Ⓙ ✶ 10 ERRORS ✶

LESSON 86

A

1	**2**	**3**	**4**
investigate	classrooms	donkey	chart
business	horseback	students	amazement
detective	salesman	playground	cheating
company	typewriter	blinked	spun
machine		lemon	post
office			

5	**6**	**7**
blindfolded	mowed	**Vocabulary words**
trackers	Bonnie	1. peel
however	investigator	2. talent
Bertha	typing	3. report
peanuts	Sanchez	4. investigate
		5. peek
		6. sense

B

Bertha Has a Great Sense of Smell Ⓐ

If you looked at Bertha, you wouldn't notice anything strange about her. She was tall for a fourteen-year-old girl, but there's nothing strange about that. Ⓑ Also, she always had peanuts and chewing gum with her. But there's nothing very strange about that either. Ⓒ However, she was the only person in her high school who could do one thing. Ⓓ In fact, she was the only human being in the whole world who could do it.

Bertha could smell. Ⓔ She could use her nose to tell where things were, what they were, and who they were. Ⓕ ❀ 2 ERRORS ❀

Hound dogs can smell like this. A good hound dog like a beagle can track somebody. You give the dog something the person had worn, and the hound dog sniffs the trail that person left. Some hound dogs are amazing trackers. Ⓖ But the best hound dog in the world would seem to have no nose at all compared to Bertha. Ⓗ

Let's say that you tried to sneak up behind

Bertha when she was studying. Before you could get within ten meters of her she would say, "Hi." Ⓘ She would know that you were there. She would know who you were. She would know exactly where you were standing. And she would know all these things through her sense of smell.

To give you an idea of how great Bertha's sense of smell was, here's something that happened four summers ago. A bunch of her friends were at a party, and they were playing Pin the Tail on the Donkey. Ⓙ To play that game, they put up a picture of a donkey without a tail. Then they put a blindfold on you. Ⓚ They spin you around, give you a donkey's tail with a pin on one end, and let you try to stick the pin on the picture of the donkey. Four people had a turn before Bertha. One pinned the tail on a post. Another one pinned the tail on the wall that was farthest from the donkey. Ⓛ And two other players put the tail on the same wall as the picture, but their tails were still far from the donkey. Ⓜ Now it was Bertha's turn. They blindfolded her, spun her around, and handed her a tail. Ⓝ She walked over to the picture of the donkey and pinned the tail exactly on the rear end.

"Oh, come on," one of the boys said. "You're not blindfolded. You can see." Ⓞ

The others agreed that Bertha had been peeking. So they put a heavy blindfold on her, and she tried it again. Ⓟ She pinned the tail on the exact spot.

Her friends started saying she was cheating, and Bertha got a little angry. She said, "Cheating?" She faced the wall. "I'll show you something."

While she faced the wall and the others stood behind her, she started to tell what each person was doing. "Vern is standing next to the post. Fran is showing Judy something that's in her purse. Rodney is to my right. He has his hands folded behind his head." She continued to tell what every person in the group was doing. Ⓠ

Everybody looked at her in amazement. Ⓡ "How do you do that?" they asked. She explained that she did it with her sense of smell.

All the students told stories about Bertha and her sense of smell. Ⓢ Some of the stories were true, and some were not. But one day, the school tester called Bertha in for some tests. He had heard stories about her, and he wanted to see how smart she was and how well she could see and hear.

First he tested her eyes. (T) After she read the letters on a wall chart, he tested her sense of smell. (U) He said, "I'm going to give you cans that have tiny holes in the top. Sniff each can, and see if you can tell what's inside." (V)

The first can had lemon in it. Before he took the can from his case, Bertha said, "It's a lemon. It's mostly the peel with some juice. The lemon was grown in Texas. It's a thick-skinned lemon."ⓦ

The tester blinked four times and looked at Bertha and then looked at the can.ⓧ He reached for the next can, but before he could pick it up, she said, "That's a water lily. It's a very dark pink flower that was picked about three days ago."ⓨ

After the test, there were many stories about Bertha and her sense of smell.

Bertha was sorry that she had let people know about her talent.ⓩ She didn't like it when her teachers whispered about her. And she didn't like it when her friends treated her as if she was strange. Bertha wanted to be like everybody else. But during that summer when she was fourteen years old, things changed. She was really glad that she had her sense of smell. In the next story, you'll find out why.Ⓐ

 ❀ 13 ERRORS ❀

LESSON 87

A

1
refinery
equipment
honest
insist
clue
lawyer

2
company
detective
business
businesses
office

3
crime
shrugged
law
investigator
Sanchez

4
kidding
Bonnie
mowed
feelings

5
lazy
lazier
horseback
study
classrooms

6
pipeline
motor
motorcycle
heater
watering

7
machine
porch
typing
crude

8
Vocabulary words
1. normally
2. salesman
3. typewriter
4. well
5. creek
6. investigate
7. report

B Bonnie Gets a Job as an Investigator Ⓐ

The weeks just before the summer vacation went very slowly for Bertha. Ⓑ It seemed that summer would never come.

The classrooms got very hot during the last week of school. Ⓒ But suddenly school was out for the summer, and suddenly Bertha didn't have anything to do. Ⓓ She didn't have to go to class. She didn't have to get up as early in the morning. She didn't have to study. For a couple of days, she didn't do much of anything. She just felt empty. Ⓔ She went to the pool, visited with her friend Tina, and went horseback riding. She ate more peanuts than she normally ate, and she felt a lot lazier than she normally did. 🌸 2 ERRORS 🌸

About a week after summer vacation had begun, she was sitting on her front steps trying to think of something new to do. Ⓕ She noticed that her new neighbor was walking to her car. The neighbor's name was Bonnie Sanchez. "Where are you going?" Bertha asked.

Bonnie replied, "I'm going to start my new job today." Ⓖ Bonnie walked toward Bertha.

Bertha stood up and said, "What is your new job?"

"I am an investigator." Bonnie smiled and looked very proud of herself, but Bertha didn't know what an investigator does. So she asked, "What does an investigator do?"

"An investigator investigates," Bonnie replied, and she laughed. "I have a job with a state office. I investigate businesses that do not follow the law." Ⓗ

Bertha wasn't sure what that meant. She shrugged. Bonnie laughed. Then she said, "Here's how it works. Let's say that you buy a car. Let's say the salesman lies about the car. When you find out you were cheated, you call the state and tell what happened. Then I go out and investigate. When I investigate, I try to find out what really did happen, and I try to find out if the salesman broke any laws." Ⓘ

"Wow," Bertha said, "that sounds like a lot of fun. I wish I was going with you."

But Bertha did not go with her, at least not on that day. Ⓙ Bonnie got in her car and drove off to work. And Bertha didn't see her for two days. But on Friday, Bertha was coming back from the pool, and there was Bonnie, sitting on her porch. She had a little table set up, and she was typing something. Ⓚ Bertha didn't want to bother her, but she wanted to find out what Bonnie was typing.

"I can't figure this one out," Bonnie said, "and I have to finish my report today. I don't think I'm a very good investigator." She shook her head and looked back at the paper in her typewriter. Ⓛ

Bertha asked, "Can you tell me what you're typing?"

"Sure," Bonnie said. "Somebody told us that a large oil company is breaking the law. The person said that the company is taking water from a creek that runs next to the company's land. ⓜ The company is supposed to take water from deep wells that are on the company's land." ⓝ

Bonnie showed Bertha a map. The dark part of the map was the land owned by the oil company. The creek that Bonnie was investigating was east of the oil company's land. ⓞ

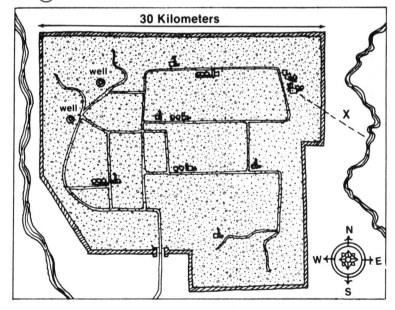

Bertha looked at the map and then laughed. "When you talked about an oil company, I thought you were talking about a little gas station. This is a place that makes gasoline." Ⓟ

"Yes," Bonnie said. "They take the oil that is pumped from the ground, and they change it into gasoline."

Bonnie tapped the place on the map that was marked with an X. "This is the place where the problem is," Bonnie said. Ⓠ "The dotted line shows an old pipe that goes from the creek to the oil plant. Ⓡ The people who run the oil company tell me that they don't use this pipe to take water from the creek. They say they haven't used the pipe in ten years." Bonnie shook her head. "I don't believe them, but I can't prove that they are taking water from the creek." Ⓢ

Bertha said, "I think I can help you." Ⓣ

❀ 11 ERRORS ❀

LESSON 88

A

1	2	3	4
Mr. Daniels	honest	heater	narrow
sign	refinery	motorcycle	twenty
guard	machine	crude	silently
recognize	lawyers	pipeline	doctors
elevator	watering	motor	drugs
medicine			
guess			

5	6	7
typists	friendly	approach
fairly	unfriendly	office
fifth	polite	approached
prison	several	offices

8
Vocabulary words
1. cock your head
2. equipment
3. explain
4. insist
5. clues

B Oil Wells

A well is a deep hole in the ground. Most wells have pipe in them so the hole stays open. Ⓐ

There are different types of wells.

• Some wells are fresh-water wells. These wells pump fresh water from under the ground. Ⓑ

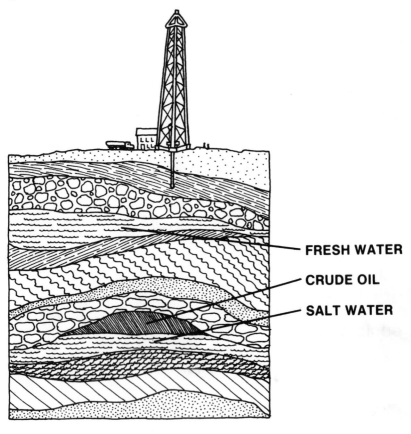

FRESH WATER

CRUDE OIL

SALT WATER

- Some wells are oil wells.
These wells pump crude oil from under the ground. Ⓒ

The picture on page 108 shows a machine that is drilling a hole for a well. Ⓓ

If the machine keeps drilling, what type of liquid will it reach first? Ⓔ

If the machine keeps drilling past the fresh water, what kind of liquid will it reach next? Ⓕ

If the machine keeps drilling, what will it reach after the oil? Ⓖ

If the well is an oil well, it pumps crude oil from the ground. Crude oil is a dark liquid that can be changed to make things like gasoline, motor oil, and plastic. Ⓗ

The crude oil is pumped from the well. Then it goes into a pipeline. Ⓘ The pipeline goes along the ground and carries the crude oil many kilometers to a refinery. Ⓙ

The refinery is a large place with strange-looking equipment and large tanks for holding oil.

The refinery changes crude oil into gasoline and other things. Ⓚ

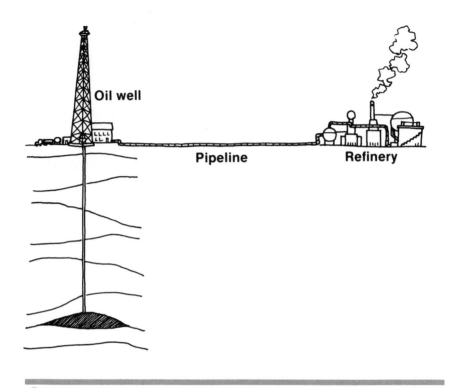

Oil well

Pipeline

Refinery

C

Bonnie Tests Bertha's Talent Ⓐ

Bertha had a plan for helping Bonnie figure out where the water came from. You probably know what her plan was. Ⓑ Although Bertha didn't know too much about oil wells and refineries, she did know that she could smell the difference between water taken from the creek and water taken from water wells. Ⓒ

Bertha was sitting on Bonnie's porch. She said, "Bonnie, it's easy for me to tell if the water comes from the creek or from the well. I'll just smell it."

Bonnie looked slowly at Bertha and made a face. "What are you talking about?" **(D)**

Bertha said, "Take me with you, and I'll tell you where the water comes from." *2 ERRORS*

Bonnie made another face. "How will you know where it comes from?"

"I told you. I'll smell it," Bertha said. Then she explained her talent. **(E)** "I can tell about anything by smelling it. Honest I can."

Bonnie cocked her head and looked at Bertha. **(F)** "What is this, a joke?" Bonnie asked.

Bertha said, "Give me a test. Get glasses of water from different places. I'll tell you where you got each glass of water." At first Bonnie didn't want to do it. "This is crazy," she kept saying. But Bertha kept insisting on the test. **(G)** Finally Bonnie went into her house and came back with three glasses of water. She said, "You can't feel them, or you may get some clues about where I got them." **(H)**

Bertha said, "I don't have to feel them. The one on the left is from your water heater. **(I)** The middle glass is from a watering can or something like that. Ⓙ That water has been sitting out for a couple of days. The water in the last glass came from a water jug or something in your refrigerator. It's been in the refrigerator for a long time, and it probably doesn't taste very good."

"I don't believe this," Bonnie said, and she tasted the water from the last glass. She made a face. "Oh, you're right. It's bad." Ⓚ

Suddenly Bonnie laughed, turned around, and looked at Bertha. She said, "I don't believe this." Then she said, "I don't believe this," three or four more times. "You're amazing. You are amazing. You are the most amazing person I have ever seen."

She kept talking very fast. She told about some of the amazing things that she had seen — a cow with two heads and a waterfall half a kilometer high. Finally, she said, "I once saw a man jump a motorcycle over twenty cars and that was amazing, but you are five times as amazing." Ⓛ

"Can I go with you?" Bertha asked.

"Yes, yes, yes, yes, yes," Bonnie said. "This will be great." Ⓜ ❁ 7 ERRORS ❁

LESSON 89

A

1	2	3	4
secretary	Mr. Daniels	signs	fifth
pretend	guessed	offices	fairly
ceiling	medicine	polite	drugs
interesting	elevator	prison	doctors
doubt	guard	unfriendly	silently
vehicle			

5	6	7
appear	cola	**Vocabulary words**
fancy	twenty	1. stretch
fancier	easy	2. approach
appeared	uneasy	3. several
speck	narrow	4. lawyers
		5. typist
		6. recognize

B

Bonnie and Bertha Go to the Oil Refinery ⒶA

A high fence stretched around Reef Oil Refinery. ⒷB Signs on the fence warned: KEEP OUT. The fence stretched as far as Bertha could see.  Bertha was sitting next to Bonnie in the front seat of the car as it moved down a narrow road. They had been driving for over an hour. Finally, the road turned to the right and came to a large gate. Bonnie drove to the gate and stopped. Ⓓ

A guard approached the car. He said, "What can I do for you?" Bertha noticed that the guard was wearing a gun. 🌀 2 ERRORS 🌀

Bonnie replied, "We're from the state. We're here to investigate a report about the water you are using."

The guard said, "One moment, please. I'll check with the main office." **Ⓔ**

As the guard walked to a little building next to the gate, Bertha said, "Wow, this place is like a prison." **Ⓕ**

Bonnie said, "The first time I came here, I had to wait for over twenty minutes before they let me in."

*Bertha watched the guard as he talked on the phone. He nodded several times and said something, but Bertha couldn't hear what he said. She knew that he was very angry, however. **Ⓖ** When people became angry they gave off a smell that was easy for Bertha to recognize.

The guard walked back to the car. He smiled and said, "Stay on the main road to building C. Mr. Daniels will meet you there." Bertha knew that the guard was still angry. **Ⓗ**

Bonnie drove slowly past the high fence and down a long road. Far down the road was a group* of tiny specks. The specks were buildings.Ⓘ One of the specks was building C.

Ten minutes later, the car was close to building C.Ⓙ Building C was very large. Bertha looked up and counted five floors. There were large windows on the top floor.Ⓚ

Another guard motioned to Bonnie, showing her where to park.Ⓛ Before the car had stopped, the guard was standing next to it. "If you will follow me, I'll take you to Mr. Daniels."

The guard was polite, but he was also angry. And he didn't like Bonnie.Ⓜ

Bertha was beginning to wonder if it was a good idea for her to be with Bonnie. When she and Bonnie had talked about it on Bonnie's porch, the idea had seemed great.Ⓝ But now, Bertha was a little frightened. She felt almost like she was having a bad dream. Here she was in this strange place, miles from anything. And the people wore guns and smelled of anger.Ⓞ

"Right this way," the guard said and led Bonnie and Bertha through the front of the building and toward the elevator.

As the elevator moved silently toward the top floor, Bertha's nose was very busy. There was a restaurant on the second floor. One of the things being served was fish. Another was roast beef. The third floor had offices on it. And there were lawyers on the third floor. Bertha could always tell lawyers' offices because their books have a strange smell. The books that doctors use have the same kind of smell, but doctors' offices also smell of medicine and drugs.

The fourth floor had a lot of typists on it. Most of them were fairly young women. Bertha could tell by the kind of clothes they wore and the make-up they used.

The fifth floor was the top floor. Bertha guessed that there weren't more than ten people on the whole floor. This floor was where the top people in the Reef Oil Refinery worked, and there was something cold and unfriendly about the fifth floor. Ⓟ ❈ 10 ERRORS ❈

LESSON 90

A

1	2	3	4
weather	interesting	sweaty	bucket
garage	ceiling	fancier	winked
dozen	secretary	buzzer	liar
respond	shrugged	cola	ducked
excused	vehicle		
demand			

5

stare
staring
faint
faintly

6

Vocabulary words

1. beyond a doubt
2. pretend
3. fancy
4. appear
5. uneasy

B

Bonnie and Bertha Meet Mr. Daniels Ⓐ

With a whisper, the doors of the elevator opened.Ⓑ And there was the fifth floor. A woman was standing in front of the elevator door. "Hello," she said, smiling. Her smile was real, and she was not angry.Ⓒ "I'm Mr. Daniels's secretary, Donna."

"Hi," Bertha said, feeling better to be near somebody who was not pretending to be polite.Ⓓ

Donna led Bertha and Bonnie to a very fancy office, with thick rugs and windows that went up the walls and continued across part of the ceiling.Ⓔ

"Would you care for a soft drink or anything?" Donna asked. 2 ERRORS

"Yes, thank you," Bertha said.

Donna left the office. Bertha said, "What a huge office."

"Yeah," Bonnie said. "This place makes me feel funny." (F)

For a few moments Bertha stood in the middle of the room, feeling very small. (G)

Donna appeared again. (H) "Here you are," Donna said, holding a large glass of orange juice.

"Oh, thanks," Bertha said.

Just then a buzzer sounded from a desk in the far corner of the office. (I) "That's Mr. Daniels," Donna said, and walked very quickly to her desk. "Yes, Mr. Daniels?" she said into a speaker.

"You may send them in." (J)

Before Bertha knew it, she and Bonnie were being led into an office that was even larger and fancier than the one they had been in. (K) Bertha was very busy, looking, listening, and sniffing. (L)

"I'm Mr. Daniels," a voice said. The smell

told Bertha that he was very angry. But his face was smiling as he approached Bonnie and Bertha.Ⓜ

"Hi," Bertha said. She realized that she was still holding her juice. She almost spilled it as she reached to shake hands with Mr. Daniels. He was a tall man, wearing a gray suit. His head was almost bald, but he didn't look very old. His hand was sweaty.Ⓝ

He looked at Bonnie. "Now, then, Miss Sanchez," Mr. Daniels said in a smooth voice.Ⓞ He continued, "What brings you back to visit us? I thought we had answered all your questions about the water."Ⓟ

Bonnie said, "I have some more questions. This time I brought along Bertha, who may give us the answers. She can tell beyond a doubt where the water comes from."Ⓠ

Mr. Daniels's face seemed to become hard.Ⓡ "I don't like this," he said. His anger was beginning to show in his face, which was turning redder. "We do a lot of work with the state, and we have always tried to be good to people from the state." His voice was quite loud.

"I'm sorry," Bonnie said. "I'm an

investigator, and I have to do my job.''

"Then do it,'' Mr. Daniels said sharply.Ⓢ Mr. Daniels walked from the office.

Before Bertha could ask, "What do we do now?'' Donna came into the room. Bertha could tell that she felt very uneasy. "I'm to take you to building 9,'' she said. "You will see the water in that building.''Ⓣ

"Is that where they use the water?'' Bonnie asked.

"I think so,'' Donna said. She was lying. When people lie, they give off a special smell.Ⓤ

❋ 8 ERRORS ❋

LESSON 91

A

1	**2**	**3**	**4**
adventure	excused	faintly	swoop
chief	garage	staring	clover
comfortable	weather	liar	complain
arrange	ducked	winked	complaint
factory		bucket	swooped
practice			

5

Vocabulary words

1. dozen
2. respond
3. demand
4. expression
5. vehicles

B **Bertha Tests Some Water** Ⓐ

The drive to building 9 was probably five kilometers. On the way, Donna tried to be friendly. She talked about the weather and about what she planned to do next month when she went on her vacation. But Bertha's nose told her that Donna felt very uneasy.Ⓑ

Building 9 looked like a giant garage.Ⓒ More than a dozen trucks and cars were parked inside.Ⓓ Workers were working on three of the vehicles.Ⓔ

As Bertha and Bonnie left Donna's car, Donna said, "I've got to go back to my desk. Big Ted will take care of you. He's the head of this garage." ✿ 2 ERRORS ✿

Big Ted was one of the biggest people Bertha had ever seen. The top of Bertha's head was only a little higher than his belt. Ⓕ "You want water, you've got water," Big Ted announced in an unfriendly way. He turned around, picked up a bucket full of water and placed it on the floor in front of Bonnie. Some water spilled over the side of the bucket. "Water, water," Big Ted said smiling. "You want it, we've got it." He turned around and winked at one of the other men. Ⓖ

Bertha said, "Where did you get this water?"

Big Ted said, "From the refinery, of course."

Bertha said, "And how did the water get to the refinery?"

"From a well," responded Ted, without smiling. Ⓗ

"Not so," Bertha said. "This water came from that truck over there." She pointed to a tank truck that had the words REEF OIL REFINERY painted on it. Ⓘ "And that truck got the water from a place that must be 30 kilometers south of here. It's from a stream that leads to the ocean. Ⓙ It did not come from a well.''

"Hey," Ted shouted. "Who is this kid?" He bent down so that his face almost touched Bertha's. "Are you calling me a liar?" Ⓚ

Bertha swallowed. Ⓛ Some of the men who had been working on the vehicles were staring. Bertha looked down. Her heart was pounding. With all her power she made herself say this: "I don't mean to call you a liar. I'm just telling you where the water came from."

"Don't pick on her," Bonnie shouted. Her voice echoed through the large garage. "She's telling the truth and you know it!" Ⓜ

Big Ted stared at Bonnie. Then he smiled. "Okay, okay," he said. "The kid looks at water and can tell where it comes from. You believe her instead of me. If that's what you want to do, I'm not going to stop you."

Ted walked to a man standing by the phone. "Call Daniels," Ted said. "Tell him to get down here <u>right now</u>." Ⓝ

Ted smiled. "If you <u>girls</u> will excuse me, I've got other things to do." Ⓞ

Ted walked away, and Bertha and Bonnie

were once more standing all alone in the middle of the huge garage. None of the workers looked at them. Nobody talked to them. (P)

Within ten minutes, Donna's car pulled up in front of the building. Mr. Daniels got out of the car. "What's the problem?" he said as he walked toward Bonnie.

"Plenty," Bonnie shouted. Bertha didn't know that Bonnie could shout that loudly. The workers stopped and began to stare again. "What kind of tricks are you trying to pull?" Bonnie demanded. (Q) Before Mr. Daniels could answer, she continued, "You bring us out here to a garage and show us some water that you brought in by truck. Why don't you just take us to the place where you are using the water? Let us test that water."

"Well," Mr. Daniels said, looking away from Bonnie, "I can't do that. I just can't . . . "

"Why not?" Bonnie demanded.

Mr. Daniels looked up. "You'll have to come back on another day. You cannot go to the refining buildings today."

"Just a minute," Bonnie said. "If you throw us out, I'm coming back with the police. I'm an investigator for the state, and you better remember that.''

Mr. Daniels turned around and smiled faintly.Ⓡ He didn't say a word, but his expression was filled with hate. He ducked into Donna's car, and the car moved slowly down the road.Ⓢ ✼ 11 ERRORS ✼

LESSON 92

A

1	2	3	4
shadow	twenty	factories	breathe
aware	sticky	chief	purple
objected	dizzy	clover	tingles
	study	swooped	upper
			faint

5

Vocabulary words

1. adventure
2. complaint
3. comfortable
4. arranged
5. practiced

B

Bonnie and Bertha Make Up a New Plan Ⓐ

Bertha wanted to tell everybody about her adventure, but nobody was around. Ⓑ Tina was swimming and Judy wasn't around. Even Bertha's mother was out of the house. Ⓒ

After making five phone calls, Bertha went over to Bonnie's house. The windows were open, and Bertha could see Bonnie talking on the phone. "But, chief," she said, "I didn't force my way into anybody's office.(D) . . . No, I did not call Daniels a crook.(E) . . . That's a lie, chief. I didn't say anything like that to Big Ted."(F) At last Bonnie hung up the phone and walked outside, shaking her head.(G) ❋ 2 ERRORS ❋

"That Mr. Daniels called up my office and told a lot of lies," Bonnie said. "And the chief believes him. The chief told me that if there's one more complaint, I'll have to turn this investigation over to another investigator."(H)

"I've got an idea," Bertha said. "Why don't you get your chief to go out there with us?"

"Oh, no," Bonnie said. "That will never work."

"Why not?"

"Well, for one thing, you're not a state investigator, and I'll have trouble explaining why you're going along."

"Oh, that's right," Bertha said. Bertha looked up at the sky. Three white fluffy clouds were so bright that they hurt her eyes. Three birds moved across the sky, landing in a huge tree on the next block. The smells of summer were heavy. Someone had just mowed a lawn on the next block. The grass had a lot of clover in it. Ⓘ

"I've got it," Bertha said suddenly. "Oh, boy." She began to do a little dance. Ⓙ Bertha said, "Listen to this idea. It's great. You get your chief to go with you. And I hide in the trunk of your car. You just make sure that the car is near the refinery. Bring a jar of water from the refinery to the car. Tap on the trunk of the car, and I'll tell you where the water comes from." Ⓚ

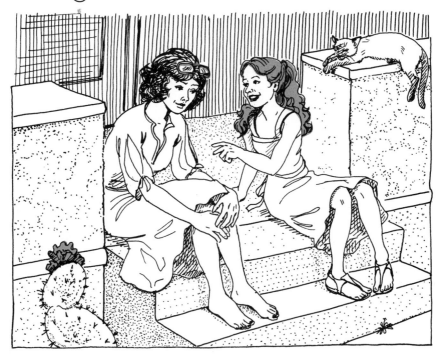

"No," Bonnie said. "That will never w——."
She stopped talking and slowly smiled. Ⓛ
Bonnie said, "I'll bet it <u>will</u> work. I think that's a
<u>great</u> idea." She began to laugh. "We'll get that
Mr. Daniels yet." Ⓜ

●　　　　●　　　　●

It was dark inside the trunk of Bonnie's car.
And it wasn't very comfortable, but Bonnie had
given Bertha three pillows. Bertha had
arranged them so that one was under her head,
while the others were under her body. Ⓝ Bertha
didn't need her eyes to know where the car was.
By using her nose, she could tell when the car
was at the corner of Fifth and Main, when the
car went past the factories on Main, and when
the car was outside the city. Bertha knew nearly
as much about where she was as she would
have known if she could have used her eyes.

The smell of the refinery gave Bertha an
uneasy feeling. Ⓞ She remembered the anger
that came from most of the people at the Reef Oil
Company. Bonnie also felt uneasy. Bertha could
tell from the smells that came from the car.
Bonnie's chief did not feel uneasy. He gave off
the smell of somebody who is sleepy. Ⓟ

The car came to a stop at the gate, and Bertha could hear voices. She had trouble understanding what they said, and she began to wonder how loudly she would have to talk for Bonnie to hear her. They probably should have practiced talking to each other when Bertha was in the trunk, but Bonnie had been a little late that morning so they had had no time to practice. Ⓠ

The voice outside the car said something about Mr. Daniels. Did the voice say that Mr. Daniels would come to the gate? Bertha wasn't sure. Ⓡ She rolled over and tried to press her ear to a crack in the trunk, but nobody was talking now.

As Bonnie's car waited at the gate, the trunk began to fill with new smells, the smells of heat. The sun beat down on the car, and the inside of the trunk got hotter and hotter. Ⓢ Bertha rolled over again and tried to find a comfortable spot. It was getting so hot inside the trunk that Bertha was starting to feel a little sick. Ⓣ ❀ 11 ERRORS ❀

LESSON 93

A

1	2	3	4
objected	tingles	sticky	brand
shadows	purple	studied	wood
aware	dizzy	twenty-one	cottonwood
half-aware	breathe	confused	bumper
upper			

5

Vocabulary words

1. make sense
2. in a fog
3. half-aware
4. faint

B

Inside a Hot Trunk Ⓐ

Bonnie's car was waiting at the gate, and Bertha was starting to feel sick from the heat inside the trunk. At last, a voice outside the car said, "Drive to building twenty-one. To get there, keep right." Ⓑ The voice continued to give directions. Bertha didn't hear the rest of the directions.ⓒ

Bertha was starting to talk out loud. "Let's go," she said. "Let's get moving."ⓓ She didn't talk loud enough for anybody outside the car to hear her. But she knew that if the car was moving, the air in the trunk wouldn't stay so hot. At least, she hoped that the air wouldn't stay so hot. "Let's go."ⓔ ✲ 2 ERRORS ✲

The car went to building twenty-one. Bertha could tell by the smells that building twenty-one was near many other buildings. The smell of oil was so strong that anybody could smell it.ⓕ Building twenty-one was one of the buildings that refined the crude oil.ⓖ

The car doors opened.ⓗ Bonnie and the chief got out of the car. They talked to two men. Bertha knew that one of these men was Mr. Daniels. She didn't know the other man.ⓘ

Suddenly, Bertha realized that Bonnie had parked the car in the sun. The temperature inside the trunk was going up. It was already so hot that Bertha couldn't stand it. The air seemed thick and hard to breathe. Now it was getting even hotter. Bertha was starting to breathe hard.Ⓙ Her body was wet and sticky.

The voices outside faded as Bonnie and the others went into building twenty-one.Ⓚ For a long time nothing happened, except the heat continued to pound against Bertha. Suddenly, Bertha caught the smell of Bonnie. She was near the car, but she wasn't alone. The man that had been with Mr. Daniels was next to Bonnie.

Water. Yes, there was the smell of water. Bonnie was holding a container of water close to the trunk of the car.Ⓛ

Bertha heard the man say something about going back inside. Bonnie answered in a loud voice, "I want to look at the water in the sunlight." Bertha knew that was a lie.Ⓜ

The water was from the creek.Ⓝ But Bertha couldn't say anything while the other man was around.

"Wow!" Bertha said out loud. She was starting to feel dizzy. Her hands and feet felt strange. She was starting to see purple dots that she knew were not actually there.Ⓞ

Then, without knowing it, she yelled out, "Near the barn." She was only half-aware that she said anything.(P) The words didn't make any sense to her, and she didn't know what made her say them. She was in a fog made up of purple dots, tingles, and a feeling that everything was falling, falling.(Q)

•   •   •

The trunk was open, and the hot sun was beating against Bertha.(R) Two forms were close to her. One was Bonnie. Her face was very close to Bertha's. Her mouth was moving and sounds were coming from it. Bertha noticed that Bonnie had a little scar on her upper lip.(S) ". . . all right? Are you all right?" Bonnie's voice said.

". . . trying to do?" the man's voice said angrily.(T) "What are you trying to do here? Who is this girl? I'm getting Mr. Daniels right now."

Bertha sat up. Bonnie's arms were around her. Bertha was starting to feel better. "I'm sorry," she said. "I think I fainted from the heat."

"It's all right," Bonnie said. "Don't try to talk. Just take it easy for a few minutes."

Three men walked quickly from building twenty-one—Mr. Daniels, the chief, and the man who had been with Bonnie.

That man said, "She was in the trunk of the car. I don't know what they are trying to do."

The three men stopped near the trunk. Two of their shadows fell on Bertha. Ⓤ Bonnie's chief said, "Bonnie, what is this all about?"

 10 ERRORS

LESSON 94

1	2	3	4
permitted	bumper	confused	fair
immediately	objected	bench	unfair
unless	brand	hood	cloth
consultant	studied	list	cost
require			

5

Vocabulary words

1. cottonwood trees
2. object to something
3. weak
4. study
5. required

B **Underlined Words**

Some of the words in the story you will read today must be spoken loudly. Here's the rule about words that must be spoken louder than other words: **The words that must be spoken louder are underlined.** Ⓐ

Below are sentences with underlined words. Say the underlined words in a loud voice. Say the other words in a soft voice. Ⓑ

a. That is <u>wrong</u>. Ⓒ
b. You are a <u>crook</u>.
c. I am <u>not</u> a crook.
d. I'm <u>tired</u> of reading.
e. My name is <u>Sam</u>.
f. <u>My</u> name is Sam, <u>too</u>.
g. This book is <u>hard</u>.
h. If you think <u>your</u> book is hard, try reading <u>this</u> book.
i. You sure like to <u>talk</u>.

C

The Chief Listens to Bertha Ⓐ

Bertha was lying in the open trunk of Bonnie's car. Ⓑ The shadows were cool, but the sun was very bright and hot. Next to the car was a group of people. The chief asked why Bertha had come along. Bonnie was trying to explain. "Chief," she said, "Bertha can tell us exactly where the water comes from. I knew that you might not let her come along because she doesn't work for the state. So what I did was . . ." Ⓒ

*Suddenly, everybody seemed to be talking at once, and their shadows moved around. Ⓓ For one moment Bertha would feel cool in their shadows. The next moment, she would feel the terrible heat of the sun. Ⓔ ❋ 2 ERRORS ❋

Mr. Daniels was saying something about the state bringing <u>kids</u> out to an oil refinery. Ⓕ The man who was with Mr. Daniels kept asking, "What kind of trick is the state trying to pull?"

Bonnie kept saying, "But she can tell us where the water . . ." Ⓖ

"Everybody, be <u>quiet</u>," the chief said loudly and raised his hand. "Let Bonnie answer this question: How could that girl* tell us where the water comes from?" Ⓗ

"She smells," Bonnie said, and everybody looked at her. Ⓘ There was a long moment of silence. "I mean," Bonnie said, "she smells with her nose. I don't mean she smells bad. She can smell things and tell what they are or where they are from."

The chief looked at Bertha. He gave off the smell of somebody who was not afraid but was a little confused. "Is that right?" he asked Bertha. "Can you really do that?"

Bertha was feeling better now. She nodded her head. Ⓙ

"What kinds of things can you tell about me?" he asked. Before she could answer, he continued, "Can you tell if I smoke?"

She felt weak, but she smiled. She took a deep breath. "Your socks are brand new," she said. Ⓚ "First time you wore them."

The chief didn't say anything. He just looked at her. He studied her face. Ⓛ "This is crazy," Mr. Daniels was saying. "We're trying to run a business here. We don't have time . . ." Ⓜ

The chief held up his hand again. Bertha said to the chief, "You live two kilometers south of town, near some cottonwood trees. You have a dog—a pointer, I think." Ⓝ

The chief smiled and shook his head. "That's amazing," he said. Ⓞ

"It's crazy if you ask me," Mr. Daniels said. "We're trying to run a . . ." Ⓟ

The chief sat down on the car's bumper. Ⓠ "Tell me," he said softly, "what does your nose tell you about the water they're using here?"

"Who cares what a <u>kid</u> says?" Mr. Daniels objected. The chief didn't take his eyes off Bertha. Ⓡ

"The water comes from the creek," Bertha said. "It is not well water."

"How can she tell that?" Mr. Daniels yelled. "She's calling us liars. I'm not going to stand for that. I'm going . . ."

The chief did not take his eyes off Bertha. "Are you sure?" he asked.Ⓢ

"Yes," Bertha said. "I could smell tiny plants in the water. These plants need sunlight to grow. So the water can't come from a well."

Mr. Daniels was yelling louder. "When did the state start using kids to do its business? The water is from a well, not from the creek."Ⓣ

Suddenly the chief turned around and pointed his finger at Mr. Daniels. "You be quiet. Do you understand?" The chief turned to Bonnie. "Get me six jars of water—three from the well and three from the creek."Ⓤ

"I'll have one of my men get them," Mr. Daniels said.Ⓥ

"No, thanks," the chief said. "Bonnie will get them." Mr. Daniels's face turned red.Ⓦ

✿ 10 ERRORS ✿

LESSON 95

1	2	3	4
Achilles	unless	cloth	battle
homonym	clue	shoulders	fear
Hector	cost	list	battled
chariot	magic	hood	bench
poison			feared

5	6
weak	**Vocabulary words**
weakness	**1.** permitted
box	**2.** unfair
boxer	**3.** perfect
lawyers	**4.** consultant
	5. required

B

Bertha Tests the Water Ⓐ

Half an hour later, Bertha was seated on a
long bench just outside building twenty-one of
the refinery. She was blindfolded. In fact, she
wore three blindfolds. Ⓑ The chief had stuck
tape over each eye. He had then wrapped a long
cloth around her head. Finally, he had placed a

hood over her head. The hood came down to her shoulders. ⓒ Next to her on the bench were six jars. Each was marked with a letter—A, B, C, D, E, and F. ⓓ

The chief said, "This will be a good test. There is no way that she can see through the blindfolds. ⓔ Even if she could see, she has no way of knowing where the water in each jar came from." ✿ 2 ERRORS ✿

The chief continued, "She won't be permitted to touch the jars, so she won't be able to use the water temperature as a clue.Ⓕ The only way that she'll be able to figure out where the water came from is to use her nose."Ⓖ

"I think this test is <u>unfair</u>," Mr. Daniels said. "I'm calling our lawyers, right <u>now</u>."Ⓗ

"You call your lawyers," the chief said. "But I would like you and your men to watch what happens here. I'm going to write down what Bertha says about each jar. When she's done, I'll read where the water in each jar actually came from."

The chief picked up jar A. "I'm holding jar A in front of you," the chief said.Ⓘ

"Yes," Bertha replied. "And that water comes from the creek."

"You're sure about that?" the chief asked.

"I'm very sure," Bertha replied. The chief wrote, "Jar A—creek."

The chief held up the other jars one at a time. He told the letter of the jar. Then Bertha told about the water. Then the chief wrote what she said.Ⓙ

After she had smelled all six jars, the chief told Bonnie, "Now give me the list that tells where you got each jar of water."Ⓚ

Bonnie handed the list to the chief.

He read the list to himself and smiled.Ⓛ "It seems that Bertha made a perfect score on this test.Ⓜ The water in jars A, B, and D came from the creek. The water in jars C, E, and F came from the well. That is exactly what Bertha said."

"This doesn't prove <u>anything</u>," Mr. Daniels objected.Ⓝ

"I think it proves a <u>lot</u>," the chief replied.Ⓞ "Bertha showed that she can tell where these jars of water came from. If she's right about these jars, she must be right about the water in the refinery. She says that the water in the refinery is from the creek. So that water must be from the creek."Ⓟ

The chief said to Mr. Daniels, "You are using water from the creek. That is against the law. I order this refinery closed — <u>immediately</u>."Ⓠ

"You can't <u>do</u> that," Mr. Daniels shouted.

"I just <u>did</u> it," the chief said. "And I mean <u>immediately</u>."

Bertha couldn't help but smile. The chief walked up to Bertha, put an arm around her shoulder, and walked toward the car with her.

He said, "We can't use people who don't work for the state unless they are special consultants."

"Oh," Bertha said sadly.

"Special consultants must fill out a form, and we must pay them."

"Oh," Bertha said.

"In fact, we're required to pay special consultants two hundred dollars a day." Ⓡ

"Oh," Bertha said.

"So you'd better fill out one of those forms if you want to be a special consultant. You've already worked two full days." Ⓢ

Bertha didn't want to say, "Oh," again and she didn't know exactly what to say, so she just looked up at the chief and smiled. Ⓣ She felt that she was smiling too much, but she couldn't seem to stop.

Smile, Bertha Turner. Smile. Ⓤ 10 ERRORS

LESSON 96

1	2	3
poison	Achilles	**Vocabulary words**
chariot	feared	fear
Hector	weakness	
boxer	battled	
poisoned	magic	
	homonym	

B

FORM 80
SPECIAL CONSULTANTS AND GROUP LEADERS

1. Have you worked for the state before? _____
2. How old are you? _____
3. Print your full name. _____
4. Do you want to be a special consultant or a group leader? _____
5. Do you have your own car? _____
6. How much will you earn every day? _____

7. What is your special talent? _____

8. If you are to be a group leader, answer these
   questions:
   a. How many are in your group? _____
   b. What is your special topic? _____

9. If you are to be a special consultant, answer
   this question: What's the name of the
   investigator you work with? _____

c Learning about an Achilles' Heel

Another name for a **weakness** is **Achilles'
heel.** Ⓐ Read this sentence: Her **love of candy**
was her **weakness.**

Here's a sentence that means the same
thing: Her **love of candy** was her **Achilles'
heel.** Ⓑ

Read this sentence: His **poor reading** was
his **weakness.**

Here's a sentence that means the same

thing: His **poor reading** was his **Achilles' heel.** Ⓒ

Read this sentence: The **boxer's left hand** was his **weakness.**

Say the sentence another way. Ⓓ

Read this sentence: Her **bad health** was her **weakness.**

Say the sentence another way. Ⓔ

You may wonder why the words **Achilles' heel** mean **weakness.** The story that you will read today tells why. That story took place over 3 thousand years ago. The story is about a man who was in a great war. You've already read about the war that took place 3 thousand years ago. Which war was that? Ⓕ

The man was a great soldier with the army that was at war with Troy. What army was that? Ⓖ

D　　ACHILLES' HEEL Ⓐ

This is a story about one of the Greek soldiers in the war with Troy. The name of this soldier was Achilles. Ⓑ The story about Achilles is make-believe.

When Achilles was a baby, his mother took him to a river. This river was filled with magic water. Here's the rule about the water in that river: **If the water touched a part of your body, nothing could hurt that part.** Ⓒ If the water touched your hand, nothing could hurt your hand. A knife or an arrow could not hurt your hand. If you put your leg in this magic water, what would happen to the leg? Ⓓ

❋ 2 ERRORS ❋

Achilles' mother loved her baby very much. She did not want anything to hurt him. She said, ''I will dip my baby in the magic river. Then nothing will be able to hurt Achilles.'' Ⓔ

But the water in the river moved very fast. Achilles' mother said, ''If I let go of my baby in the water, the river will carry him away. So I must hold on to part of him.'' Ⓕ Achilles' mother thought and thought about how to hold her baby when she dipped him into the river.

At last she said, ''I will hold Achilles' heel when I dip him in the magic river.'' So she did. Achilles' mother held on to his heel and dipped him in the magic river. The only part of Achilles that did not get wet in the magic river was his heel. **G**

Achilles grew up to be the greatest soldier that Greece ever had. **H** All the cities in Greece heard about Achilles, and the soldiers from these cities were afraid of him. When he was still a boy, he battled the best soldiers. They hit him with their swords, but the swords did not cut him. They shot him with arrows, but the arrows did not hurt him. When they saw that they could not kill him, they tried to run from him. But Achilles rode after them on his horse and killed them.

When the war with Troy started, Achilles was the most feared soldier in the world. **I**

 6 ERRORS

LESSON 97

1	2	3	4
homonym	ashes	scale	**Vocabulary**
needle	burnt	weigh	**words**
continue	crushed	scales	poison
Hector	chariot	weighing	
continued	poisoned		

B

Homonyms

The words with the most scars in the word bank are those that sound the same as other words. A word that sounds the same as another word is called a homonym. Ⓐ You have learned many homonyms. You have learned a homonym for the word **four**. Ⓑ The words **four** and **for** sound the same, but something is different about them. Ⓒ

You have also learned other homonyms. The word **new** has a homonym. Ⓓ The word

eight has a homonym.Ⓔ Other numbers have homonyms.Ⓕ

The sentence below has words that are homonyms: **She rode one bike from here to there.** How many homonyms can you find in the sentence?Ⓖ

Remember the name we use for words that sound the same as other words.Ⓗ

C   Chariots

During the war between Greece and Troy, people didn't have the kinds of vehicles we have today. They used horses to pull their vehicles on land. Horses pulled carts. Horses also pulled small vehicles with two wheels, called chariots.Ⓐ Soldiers used chariots in battles. Chariots could move very fast. Maybe six horses would pull the chariot. Maybe two horses would pull it.Ⓑ

Sometimes two soldiers would be in a chariot. One would steer. The other would be able to use both hands to shoot arrows or hold a shield and throw spears.

Look at the vehicle in the picture. What is

its name?Ⓒ How many wheels does it have?Ⓓ How many soldiers are in it?Ⓔ How many horses are pulling it?Ⓕ What is soldier A doing?Ⓖ What is soldier B doing?Ⓗ

If you look closely at the picture, you will see that the chariot has sharp knives on it. These knives turn around and around when the chariot moves. They would cut through anything that got in their way. Where are those knives?Ⓘ

D The Greatest Soldier Ⓐ

A thousand ships went to war with Troy.Ⓑ There were soldiers on every ship. Achilles was on one of the ships. For ten years he was in the war with Troy. The soldiers of Troy shot arrows at him and threw spears at him. But nothing hurt Achilles.Ⓒ

There was also a great soldier in the city of Troy. His name was Hector. The people of Troy said, "Hector is as fast as a deer. He is as strong as an elephant. Hector is the greatest soldier in Troy."

Achilles knew that Hector was the greatest soldier of Troy. Achilles had heard the stories about how fast Hector was and how strong he was. ❋ 2 ERRORS ❋

Achilles was getting tired of hearing people say that Hector was the greatest soldier. "I am the greatest soldier," Achilles said. "And I'll prove it."Ⓓ

Achilles went to the wall of Troy. He yelled to the men on the wall, "Send out Hector. I will fight him. We will see who is the greatest soldier."Ⓔ

Soon the huge gate opened, and a man came out. He was a huge man, carrying a great spear. "I am Hector," the soldier from Troy yelled. "I will show you who is the greatest soldier."

Hector and Achilles started to fight. The men on the wall of Troy watched. The Greek soldiers watched. Hector and Achilles fought for hours. At last Achilles won the fight.Ⓕ Hector was dead. Achilles held up his spear and said,

"I am the greatest soldier of all. Nothing can hurt me." **Ⓖ**

The soldiers of Troy shouted back at him. **Ⓗ** They could not believe that Hector had been killed. They hated Achilles. So they shouted at him and called him names. **Ⓘ**

Achilles laughed at the soldiers of Troy. Then he shouted back at them, "You would like to kill me. I will give you a chance to do that." **Ⓙ**

He took a chariot and started to ride around the wall of Troy. He stayed very close to the wall so that the soldiers of Troy could shoot arrows and throw spears. The arrows and spears bounced from his head and his chest and his legs. He laughed. "Kill me," he shouted, waving his sword at them. **Ⓚ** "Here is your chance to kill me."

By the time he was about half-way around the great wall, arrows and spears were stuck all over the chariot. One of the horses had been hit by an arrow. Spears and arrows were falling like rain on Achilles. **Ⓛ** Some of the arrows had poisoned tips. But they didn't bother Achilles. He was laughing and shaking his sword at the soldiers of Troy.

Then something strange happened. A soldier on the wall shot a poisoned arrow at Achilles. The arrow almost missed Achilles. But it hit him in the heel.**(M)** Immediately, he dropped his sword. He cried out and fell from the chariot. He tried to stand up, but then he fell over. Achilles was dead.**(N)** He had been killed because of his Achilles' heel.**(O)** 🌸 8 ERRORS 🌸

LESSON 98

1	2	3	4
skeleton	toward	scales	figure
buffalo	needle	ashes	continued
	pressed	crushed	early
	eight	burnt	earlier
	eighty	weighing	figuring

B Facts about Scales

In today's story, you'll read about weighing things on a scale. Ⓐ Here are facts about scales.

• A scale tells how much things weigh. Ⓑ

• Some scales weigh things that are not very heavy. These scales tell how many grams things weigh. Ⓒ The picture at the top of the next page shows a scale that is used to weigh 30 flies. The weight on the other side of the scale is just as heavy as the 30 flies. Ⓓ

- Some scales weigh things that are very heavy. These scales tell how many kilograms things weigh. Ⓔ

- Some scales that tell about kilograms have needles. The needle points to numbers. The numbers tell how heavy things are. Ⓕ

When the needle moves to 12, we know how heavy the thing on the scale is. Ⓖ When the needle moves to 100, we know how heavy the thing on the scale is. Ⓗ Tell about the weight of the things in the picture below. Ⓘ

A

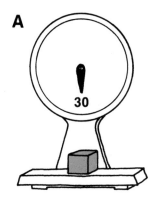

B

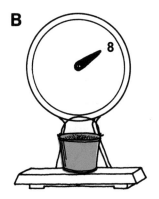

Sid Learns about Pushes in the Opposite Direction Ⓐ

Sid's dad tried to teach Sid new things, but Sid didn't like to learn new things.

One summer day, Sid and his dad went fishing. Sid was in the canoe, and Sid's dad was on the dock. Ⓑ

Sid paddled the canoe near the dock. Sid stood up in the canoe and said, "Look out, dad. I'm going to jump to the dock." Ⓒ

Sid's dad said, "Sid, if you try to jump, you will end up in the water."

"No, dad," Sid said. "I can jump that far. I'm only one meter from the dock." Ⓓ

 2 ERRORS ✿

Sid's dad said, "When you try to jump toward the dock, the canoe will move away from the dock. When something starts moving in one direction, there is always a push in the opposite direction."

"That's silly," Sid said. He laughed, and then he jumped. He jumped toward the dock as hard as he could.

What do you think happened?Ⓔ When Sid jumped, the canoe moved in the opposite direction. And, splash.Ⓕ

Sid's dad helped Sid out of the water. Then his dad said, "I told you the canoe would move in the opposite direction. When you start moving in one direction, there is always a push in the opposite direction."

"No," Sid said. "You must have made the canoe move when I jumped."Ⓖ

His dad said, "No, I didn't make the canoe move. I'll show you what happened."

Sid and his dad went to a place that had a large scale. Sid's dad said, "Stand on the scale." So Sid did. Sid's dad said, "Read the scale, and see how much you weigh when you're standing still."

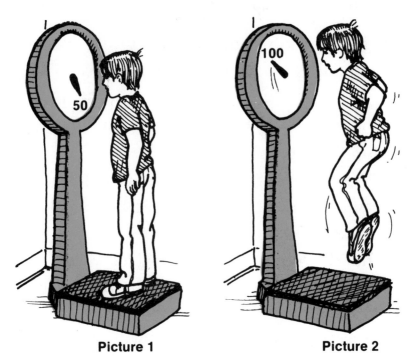

Picture 1　　　　　**Picture 2**

Sid read the scale. "The needle is pointing to 50," Sid said. "So I must weigh 50 kilograms."**Ⓗ**

His dad said, "If you jump up in the air, you'll move this way." Sid's dad pointed.**Ⓘ** "If you watch the needle, you'll see that there is a push in the opposite direction." Sid's dad pointed again.**Ⓙ**

Sid's dad continued, "Here's the rule. If you move up, there will be a push in the opposite direction. The needle on the scale will show that there is a push down. So jump up, and watch what happens to the needle."**Ⓚ**

Sid jumped, and the needle jumped at the same time. Picture 2 shows the needle on the scale when Sid jumped up. There was a push down. The needle on the scale jumped all the way to 100 kilograms. Ⓛ

Sid asked, "What happened to that scale? It went all the way to 100 kilograms when I jumped up."

His dad said, "When you started to move up, there was a push in the opposite direction. That push pressed down on the scale. It made the needle move."

Sid got on the scale and jumped up again and again. Every time he jumped up, 100 kilograms pushed down against the scale. Ⓜ

Sid thought about the push in the opposite direction.

The next time Sid and his dad went fishing, Sid did not try to jump from the canoe to the dock. He knew that if he started to move toward the dock, the push in the opposite direction would push the canoe. Ⓝ

Sid was getting smarter. ❋ 8 ERRORS ❋

LESSON 99

A

1	2	3	4
figure	expression	confused	buffalo
early	vehicle	immediately	eighty
figuring	adventure	objected	opposite
earlier	comfortable	chariot	permitted

5

Vocabulary words

1. cave
2. skeleton
3. ashes
4. kilometer
5. kilogram
6. homonym
7. dozen

Clues from Thousands of Years Ago Ⓐ

Look at the time line. It goes all the way back eighty thousand years. Touch the dot on the line that shows the war between Greece and Troy. Ⓑ

Touch the dot that shows things that happened eighty thousand years ago. Ⓒ

Now

3 thousand years ago
War between Troy and Greece

80 thousand years ago

The world was very different eighty thousand years ago. People didn't live the way they lived during the war of Troy. The people who lived eighty thousand years ago did not have chariots. They did not ride horses. They did not live in houses. They did not have bows and arrows. They did not have shields. They did not have books. They did not live in cities. **Ⓓ**

❀ 2 ERRORS ❀

Nobody who is alive today saw these people or talked to them or watched them. So how do we know anything about them? **Ⓔ**

We know about these people because they left clues. The clues tell us about what they ate and where they lived and what they did. Some clues also tell us where they died and how they died. **Ⓕ**

When you eat a big meal, you do not eat everything. You throw away some things. Let's say that you eat chicken. What parts would you throw away? **Ⓖ** Some parts of the chicken that are thrown away may last a long, long time. **Ⓗ**

Chicken bones may be a clue that somebody ate chicken. What kind of clue could tell you that somebody ate coconut? **Ⓘ**

What kind of clue could tell you that somebody ate part of a very large animal?Ⓙ

So one of the best places to look for clues about people and how they lived is their garbage pile.Ⓚ

Some garbage piles left by people who lived eighty thousand years ago are in caves.Ⓛ If we find garbage piles in caves, we have a clue about where the people ate. Where did they eat?Ⓜ

The bones in these garbage piles do not have marks from the teeth of dogs. What does that tell us about the people who lived eighty thousand years ago?Ⓝ

The garbage piles of people who lived only eight thousand years ago are different. Some bones in these garbage piles have marks from dogs' teeth.Ⓞ What does that tell us about these people?Ⓟ

*Sometimes garbage piles tell us about how animals were killed. Let's say that we found bones of a large animal like a buffalo. Let's say that these bones were broken in many places. An animal like a buffalo might get many broken bones falling from a high place. Maybe the

people who hunted these large animals chased them to a cliff and then made them run off the cliff. Ⓠ

Another thing we can tell from garbage is how the people who lived in caves fixed their food. If they made fires, some clues would be left behind. Can you think* of some? Ⓡ

Let's say we do not find any rocks with smoke and heat marks on them. And we do not find any ashes. And we do not find any burn marks on bones. These clues tell us something about how the people ate their food. Ⓢ

If we look at a garbage pile in a cave that people have used for hundreds of years, we can tell how things changed. We can tell if the people began to eat different things. Let's say we find that some of the garbage in a pile was not cooked. These things are near the bottom of the garbage pile. Let's say the things near the top of the pile were cooked. By looking at the pile, we can tell that people who lived in the cave first did not cook their food. They ate things raw. The people who lived in the same cave many, many years later began to cook food. In the next story, you'll learn the rule for getting clues from a pile. ✿ 10 ERRORS ✿

LESSON 100

A

1	2	3	4
lightning	figuring	huddle	consultant
imitate	blind	changed	required
adult	crouch	head	carrying
	blinding	overhead	animal
	crouches	huddling	together

5

Vocabulary words

1. earlier
2. homonym
3. dozen
4. kilogram
5. kilometer

B Digging into Piles Ⓐ

A garbage pile gives us clues about what happened earlier and what happened later. Here's the rule about garbage piles and all other piles: **Things near the bottom of the pile went into the pile earlier.** Ⓑ **Things near the top of the pile went into the pile later.** Ⓒ

What does the rule tell about things near the bottom of the pile? Ⓓ

What does the rule tell about things near the top of the pile? Ⓔ

Look at the picture on page 177. It shows a pile of garbage in a hole of a cave. Touch the thing labeled A and the thing labeled R. Ⓕ

❋ 2 ERRORS ❋

The thing labeled R is part of a fish. The thing labeled A is a snail's shell. The thing closer to the bottom of the pile went into the pile earlier. Which thing is that? Ⓖ

The thing closer to the top of the pile went in later. Which thing is that? Ⓗ

So the people who lived in the cave threw the fish into the garbage pile before they threw the snail into the pile.

Touch the thing labeled S and the thing labeled B.Ⓘ

What does the rule tell about things near the bottom of the pile?Ⓙ

What does the rule tell about things near the top of the pile?Ⓚ

Which letter is closer to the bottom of the pile, S or B?Ⓛ

So what do you know about thing S?Ⓜ

What do you know about thing B?Ⓝ

Touch thing A and thing S.Ⓞ

What does the rule tell about things near the bottom of the pile?Ⓟ

What does the rule tell about things near the top of the pile?Ⓠ

So what do you know about thing A?Ⓡ

And what do you know about thing S?Ⓢ

We always use the rule about piles for figuring out which things happened earlier and which things happened later.

Let's say that we come into the cave and start digging into the pile that we've just been looking at. When we start digging, the first thing we'll pick up is big bone M. Name the next thing we'll pick up.Ⓣ

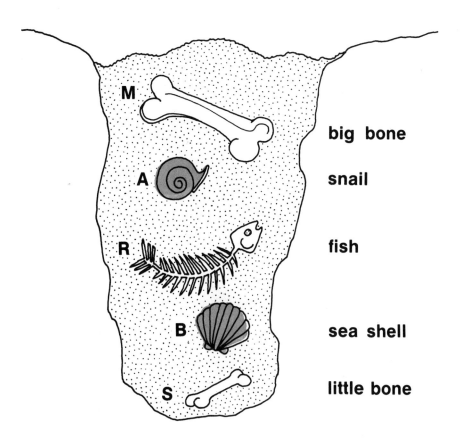

M

big bone

A

snail

R

fish

B

sea shell

S

little bone

Which of those things is closer to the bottom of the pile? Ⓤ

So which thing went into the pile earlier? Ⓥ

We've picked up thing M and thing A. What's the next thing we'll pick up? Ⓦ

Which of the things we've picked up is closest to the bottom of the pile? Ⓧ

If thing R is closest to the bottom of the pile, what else do we know about thing R? Ⓨ

What's the next thing we'll pick up?Ⓩ
Thing B is closer to the bottom of the pile.
So what else do you know about thing B?Ⓐ
A pile is like a time line. The things on top
are the last things that happened. The things at
the bottom are the things that happened first.Ⓑ
Look at the picture at the top of the next
page of a hole dug near a beach. There are small
stones at the top of the hole and mud at the
bottom of the hole. The things in this hole are
piled up. So the last things are on top and the
first things are on the bottom.
Touch the time line next to the picture.Ⓒ
Name the last thing that went into the pile.Ⓓ
Name the thing that went in just before the
small stones.Ⓔ
What went into the pile just before the
sand?Ⓕ
What went into the pile just before the
shells?Ⓖ
What was the first thing that went into the
pile?Ⓗ

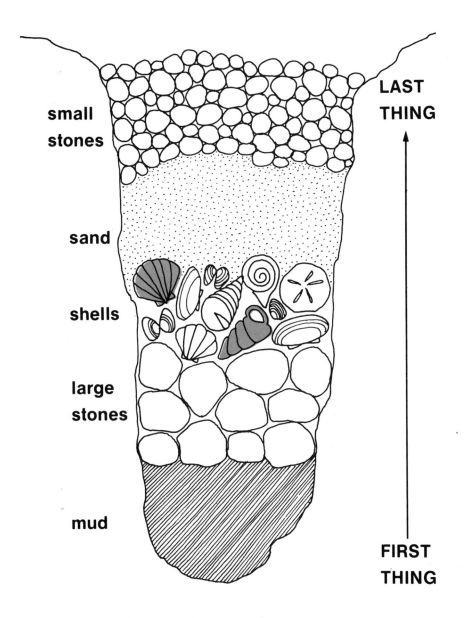

small
stones

sand

shells

large
stones

mud

LAST
THING

FIRST
THING

Here's what we find when we look at the
piles of garbage in the caves used eighty
thousand years ago.

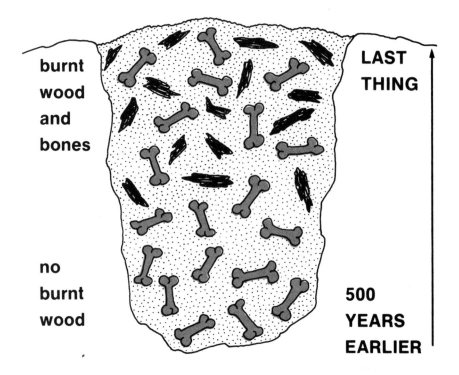

burnt
wood
and
bones

LAST
THING

no
burnt
wood

500
YEARS
EARLIER

Touch the time line. ① The time line shows that the first things went into the pile five hundred years before the last things went in. For five hundred years, people threw garbage into this pile.

Near the top of the pile are bits of burnt wood. There are no bits of burnt wood near the bottom of the pile. So we know that people in the cave did not always cook their food. The people who lived later used fire. This happened about half-way through the pile. ❀ 11 ERRORS ❀

LESSON 101

A

1	2	3
lightning	blinding	**Vocabulary words**
changed	stares	**1.** adult
huddling	pouring	**2.** huddle
crouches	imitates	**3.** thunder
	overhead	**4.** crouch

B

Fire Ⓐ

You learned a rule about piles. The rule helps you figure out which things happened earlier and which things happened later.

Say the parts of the rule that are missing: Ⓑ
Things near the bottom of the pile _____
Things near the top of the pile _____

Remember, the pile is just like a time line. The last thing that happened is on top. Where is the first thing that happened? Ⓒ

When we look at garbage piles inside caves we can figure out that the people changed the way they ate food. What kind of change took place? Ⓓ

Other clues tell us how these people lived. Some clues tell us that they wore clothes made from animal skins. Ⓔ 🌸 2 ERRORS 🌸

Some clues tell us that they used rocks and clubs to kill animals. Ⓕ You know about some clues that tell us where the people lived. Ⓖ

But the people did not stay in the same cave all the time. When the animals moved away, the people followed the animals. They found another cave to live in. Ⓗ

Get a picture of a group of these people on a cold winter day. Ⓘ The people are inside their cave. The wind is blowing outside. It's cold inside—cold. Ⓙ

Inside the cave are some children, a young baby, and some adults. Get a picture of them wrapped in their animal skins. Ⓚ Get a picture of them huddling together, trying to keep warm. Try to feel the cold, cold rocks and the cold air. Ⓛ

Now think of how important fire must have

been to these people. We don't know how these people first began to use fire. But here's how it might have happened. Ⓜ

It's raining outside the cave. Heavy clouds are low over the trees. Ⓝ It is fall and the days have been dry. Ⓞ Inside the cave, it is cool, but not cold.

CRASH, BOOM. That was the sound of thunder. Ⓟ

One of the children runs to the back of the cave and tries to hide. Ⓠ BOOM. Another great blast of thunder, and a cool wind, carrying a light spray of water. Ⓡ BOOOOOOM. That blast of thunder was very close. The clouds overhead are very dark. Two men and a woman sit near the mouth of the cave and look outside. Ⓢ Everybody else has moved to the back of the cave. Two of the people are holding their hands over their ears. Ⓣ

A silent flash of lightning as bright as the sun cuts through the sky. A moment later comes the sound of thunder that the lightning made when it cut through the air. BOOOM. Ⓤ

Another blinding flash, just outside the cave. Ⓥ The lightning works like a knife and cuts a path down the trunk of a tree. Ⓦ The lightning throws pieces of bark into the air. Ⓧ BOOOOOOOOOOOOM. The sound is so loud that the people near the front of the cave hold their hands over their ears. Ⓨ The lightning has thrown a small branch right in front of the cave. There are flames coming from one end of the branch. Ⓩ That branch is burning. Fire. The people have seen lightning fires before, but never so close. The people watch the fire for a moment. Then one of the men reaches out and tries to grab it. Ⓐ

The man licks his fingers, and the others watch the fire. **B**

Soon, all the people gather close to the fire. **C** One of the children touches the part of the branch that is not on fire. **D** Slowly, the child picks up the branch and holds it so the burning part is down. **E** The child drops the branch inside the cave and runs away from the fire. **F** A man picks up the branch and holds it so the burning end is up. **G** He smiles. The others smile. **H** They like the fire. But how are they going to keep it going? **I** ❈ 11 ERRORS ❈

LESSON 102

1	2	3
huddle	earlier	important
pouring	lightning	moment
stares	overhead	suddenly
outlines	direction	interested
hollow	figuring	tomorrow

4

Vocabulary words

1. glows
2. fire dies down
3. imitate
4. heat
5. swoop
6. club

B

Keeping the Fire Going Ⓐ

In the last story, you learned something about fire. **Fire likes to move up.** Ⓑ Which picture shows the way you should hold a

burning branch if you don't want to get
burned? ⓒ

A   B

Which picture shows the way the child held
the branch in the last story? Ⓓ

What happened when the child held the
branch that way? Ⓔ

Remember the fact about fire. Fire likes to

move up, so the heat moves up. That is an important fact that we will use in a later story.

When we left the people inside the cave, they were smiling. Why?**F**　❀ 2 ERRORS ❀

But how are they going to keep the fire going?**G**

A man is holding the burning branch. One of the children picks up a stick that is not burning and imitates the man.**H** The child is a girl about nine years old. The man holding the burning branch waves it over his head.**I** The child laughs and waves her stick over her head. The man shakes his branch. The child imitates the man.**J**

The man smiles and points his stick at the child's stick. The child points her stick at the man's stick. The ends touch.**K** When the child pulls her stick away, the end is on fire.

For a moment she stares at her stick with wide eyes.**L** Then she smiles.**M** Then everybody in the cave smiles and laughs. They pick up sticks and branches that are inside the cave and hold one end of them in the fire.**N** For a while everybody laughs and runs around with burning sticks and branches. When the sticks

burn down, some of the people get burned. Ⓞ
They drop their sticks, and they don't want to
play with the fire anymore. One of the burning
sticks falls into a pile of sticks and large
branches near the back of the cave. Ⓟ Soon,
there is a real fire in the cave. It is hot inside the
cave.

The people move outside the cave and stand
in the rain, looking inside at the fire. Ⓠ

Smoke is pouring from the cave, and the
inside of the cave is very hot.

They stand there in the rain for a long time,
until the fire dies down. Ⓡ Now the fire is a deep
red glow that is very hot. There are no high
flames coming from the fire. There is very little
smoke. But there is still a lot of heat. Ⓢ

Suddenly, a cold north wind swoops over
the hills and hits the people. They turn and face
the wind. Ⓣ The adults know this wind. It is the
first wind of winter. The night will be very cold
and the next day will be cold. There will be a
few warm days before the snow starts falling.
But winter is near, and there will be days and
days and days of cold. The adults hate the
wind. Ⓤ The adults do not want another winter.

They do not want to huddle in the cave for weeks and weeks. They do not want to go hungry for weeks and weeks. But the wind tells them that those weeks will come soon. Ⓥ

One of the adults waves his hands at the wind and makes a mean face. Ⓦ The children imitate him. Ⓧ The people are no longer interested in the fire. Slowly, they walk inside the cave. The adults know that by tomorrow that cave will be cold, cold, cold. But the cave is very warm—warm. And that warm is coming from the fire.

The people know the rules about the fire now: **If you put things on the fire, those things burn. And the fire keeps the cave warm.** Ⓨ One of the adults picks up a heavy branch and throws it on the hot, glowing fire. Ⓩ In a moment, yellow flames jump from the heavy branch. More heat goes up from the fire.

The man who waved at the wind laughs. He knows the rules about the fire. Ⓐ He knows how to keep the cave warm all winter long. Ⓑ If he keeps putting things on the fire, the fire will keep making heat. If the fire keeps making heat, how will the cave feel? Ⓒ

The man walks to the mouth of the cave and waves at the wind again. But this time, he doesn't make a mean face. He laughs at the wind. The children imitate him. The cave is warm. ❀ 12 ERRORS ❀

LESSON 103

1	2	3	4
quarter	classroom	outlines	hoof
muscle	cowboys	draft	hooves
rough	itself	grade	draw
Mongolian	baseball	graders	drawn
	basketball	racehorse	pony
	daydream		

5

Vocabulary words

1. drinking straw
2. paint
3. earth
4. hollow
5. tusks

B

CAVE PICTURES Ⓐ

The piles of garbage inside caves give us clues.Ⓑ The piles tell us what the people who lived in the caves ate. The piles also tell us that earlier cave people didn't cook their food.Ⓒ The piles aren't the only clues inside the caves.

The people made pictures on the walls of their caves. They also made outlines of their hands. The outlines give us clues about the people. Picture A shows the outlines of two hands.

PICTURE A

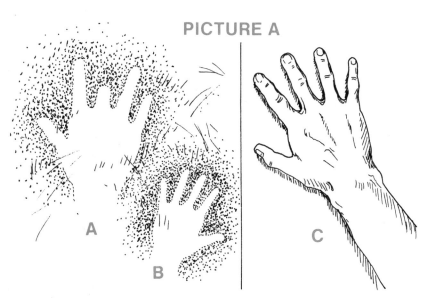

Name two things you can tell about hand A. Ⓓ

Name one thing you can tell about hand B. Ⓔ

Hand A is the hand of an adult male who lived in the cave 80 thousand years ago. Ⓕ

❋ 2 ERRORS ❋

Hand C is the hand of a full-grown man who is alive now. That man is not bigger than most other men who are alive now. Compare that hand with hand A.Ⓖ

How have adult men changed in 80 thousand years?Ⓗ

The adult men who lived in some caves 80 thousand years ago were not as tall as most women who live in the United States today.Ⓘ

Can you figure out how the people who lived in the caves made pictures of their hands?Ⓙ

Here's how the man made the picture of hand A. First he mixed up some paint.Ⓚ To make the paint, he used earth that he mixed with other things.Ⓛ By mixing earth with something like animal fat or blood, he could make red paint, black paint, brown paint, or yellow paint.Ⓜ

After he had mixed paint of the color he wanted, he put his hand against the wall of the cave. Picture B shows the man holding his hand against the wall.Ⓝ

Then he filled his mouth with the paint.

Then he put one end of a small bone in his mouth. The bone was hollow. So it worked just like a drinking straw.Ⓞ

PICTURE B

The man pointed the bone at his hand.
Picture C shows the man with the bone in his
mouth. Ⓟ

PICTURE C

Then the man blew. A stream of paint came
out of the end of the bone. Some paint went on
the man's hand. Some went on the wall. The

man kept blowing paint until the wall around his hand was covered with paint. Ⓠ

PICTURE D

Then the man pulled his hand away from the wall. And there was an outline of his hand on the wall. Ⓡ

PICTURE E

The people who lived in caves used paint to draw things other than hands.Ⓢ They painted pictures of the animals they hunted.

Picture F shows a horse and a cow.

PICTURE F

Picture G shows horses and a cow found on the wall of a cave. Compare the horses in the two pictures. Remember, cows have not changed size.Ⓣ

PICTURE G

Picture H shows a cave picture of an animal that looks like an elephant of today. No animal just like this one is alive today. Ⓤ

PICTURE H

We know that animals like the one in picture H lived thousands of years ago. Ⓥ We know about these animals because we have found the bones of large animals with very large tusks. People have put the bones together and have shown what the animal must have looked like.

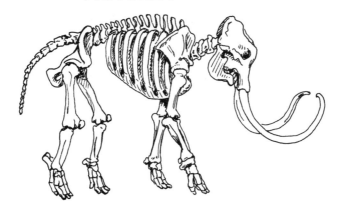

Picture I shows the bones. **W**

Picture J shows the animal that is made from the bones. Although we have never seen elephants like this one, the bones tell us how they probably looked. **X**

PICTURE J

The elephant in picture H looks a lot like the elephants must have looked. ❋ 9 ERRORS ❋

LESSON 104

A

1	2	3	4
million	daydream	quarter	hooves
eohippus	Mongolian	pony	third-graders
danger	rough	itself	draft
enough	classroom	drawn	baseball
			racehorse

5	6
lay	**Vocabulary words**
layers	**1.** hoof
size	**2.** muscles
basketball	**3.** cowboys
sized	

Different Kinds of Horses Ⓐ

Not all dogs look the same. Some are big. Some are small. Some have long hair. Some have short hair. Ⓑ

Not all horses that live today are the same. Some are bigger. Some are smaller. Some have big heavy legs. Some have thin legs. Some horses that are alive today look like the horses that lived 30 thousand years ago. Ⓒ Some types of horses that are alive today have been around for only two hundred years. Ⓓ

Picture 1 shows some types of horses.

*Horse A is a big strong horse called a draft horse. Ⓔ A draft horse cannot run as fast as some horses. But this horse is good at pulling heavy things. Ⓕ ❋ 2 ERRORS ❋

One draft horse may weigh more than all the children in a third-grade classroom. Think of that. One horse that weighs as much as 30 third-graders. Ⓖ

Horse B is a racehorse. Ⓗ Racehorses are small next to draft horses. But racehorses are fast. In a race, the racehorse runs faster than any other kind of horse. But compare the legs of the racehorse with the legs of the draft horse. Look* at their hooves and the bones right above their hooves. Ⓘ

A big racehorse may weigh half as much as a big draft horse. Ⓙ But a racehorse is big when you think that one big racehorse weighs as much as half the third-grade class. A racehorse is about 2 meters tall at the head. Ⓚ

Horse C is a quarter horse. Ⓛ Compare the quarter horse with the racehorse. Which horse has a longer back? Ⓜ Here's a surprise. The quarter horse weighs as much as the racehorse. If you want to know why, compare the hind legs of each horse. One horse has great, heavy muscles. One horse has long, slim legs. Ⓝ

Quarter horses cannot run a race as fast as racehorses, but here's the rule about quarter horses. **They can stop and turn faster than racehorses, and they are stronger than racehorses.** Ⓞ Cowboys ride quarter horses. Quarter horses are good for chasing cows and for riding over rough ground. Ⓟ

Horse D is a small horse called the Mongolian horse. Ⓠ Not many Mongolian horses

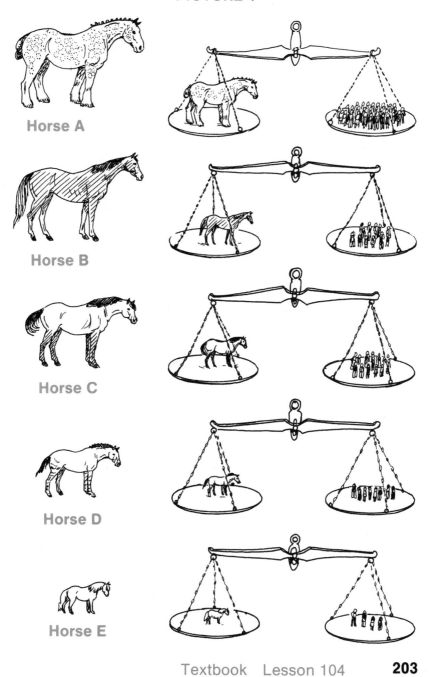

Horse A

Horse B

Horse C

Horse D

Horse E

are still alive. The Mongolian horse is much smaller than the quarter horse or the racehorse. It weighs about as much as eight third-graders.Ⓡ The Mongolian horse looks like the kind of horses drawn on the walls of caves. The Mongolian horse was the kind of horse that lived 30 thousand years ago.Ⓢ

Horse E is a pony.Ⓣ The pony is full grown, but it gets no bigger than a large dog. It is a little over a meter tall at the shoulders.Ⓤ It weighs about the same as four third-graders.Ⓥ

 7 ERRORS

LESSON 105

A

1	**2**	**3**
danger	enough	**Vocabulary words**
eohippus	thousand	**1.** in fact
layers	different	**2.** million
tusks	skeletons	
herd	earliest	

B

Horses from Millions of Years Ago Ⓐ

The people who lived in caves a long time ago drew pictures of the things around them. Ⓑ They drew pictures of elephants with huge tusks and pictures of horses. People have found bones of these horses, and the horses were small. Ⓒ

The kinds of horses that lived 30 thousand years ago are different from most of the horses that live today. Ⓓ The horses that lived millions of years ago are different from those that lived 30 thousand years ago. Over the millions of years, horses have changed a lot. Ⓔ

How do we know that horses have changed a lot? ❋ 2 ERRORS ❋

We use the rule about piles. If we look into a pile of rock, we can figure out which things came earlier. We can also figure out which things came later. Ⓕ

Look at picture 1. There is a large cliff. There are rows of stones and rocks and sea shells. Ⓖ Each row is called a layer. Ⓗ The layers are piled up. That means that the layers near the bottom of the pile came earlier than the layers near the top of the pile.

The time line next to the cliff shows how long ago each layer of rock went into the pile. Layer E went into the pile 30 thousand years ago. Layer D went into the pile 1 million years ago.

PICTURE 1

	NOW
	Story of Troy
Layer E	30 thousand years ago
Layer D	1 million years ago
Layer C	11 million years ago
Layer B	28 million years ago
Layer A	38 million years ago

When did layer C go into the pile?Ⓘ
When did layer B go into the pile?Ⓙ
When did layer A go into the pile?Ⓚ

The person who is looking at the cliff in the picture will see some things that went into the pile 11 million years ago. The person will also see some things that went into the pile more than 38 million years ago.Ⓛ

There are clues in these layers. The clues tell us about the animals that lived when each layer went into the pile. Look at layer C. It has two clues in it.Ⓜ Look at layer E. It has two clues in it.Ⓝ

When we look through layers of rock, we find skeletons of horses.Ⓞ The earliest horse skeletons are found in layer A. The skeleton of that horse is very small. In fact, it's no bigger than a beagle.Ⓟ The skeleton that is found in layer B is about as big as a pointer.Ⓠ The horse in layer C is about as big as a small pony.Ⓡ The horse in layer D is not the same size as the horse in layer C.Ⓢ The horse that is found in layer E is the horse that the cave people hunted. That horse weighed as much as 8 third-graders.

Picture 2 shows the skeletons of horses. The horse from layer A is at the bottom. Ⓣ

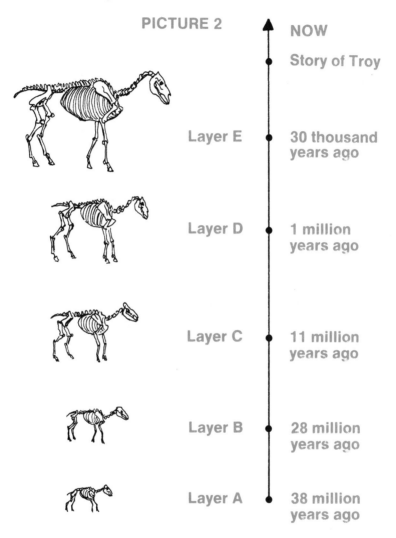

PICTURE 2

NOW

Story of Troy

Layer E · 30 thousand years ago

Layer D · 1 million years ago

Layer C · 11 million years ago

Layer B · 28 million years ago

Layer A · 38 million years ago

Look at the skeleton of the earliest horse. Then look at the skeleton of the horse from layer E. They are different in many ways. Ⓤ

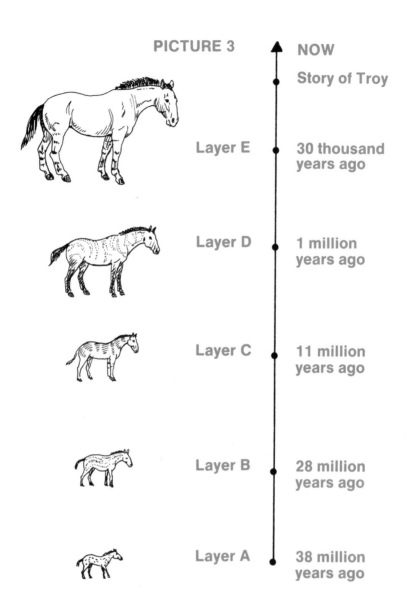

PICTURE 3

NOW

Story of Troy

Layer E — 30 thousand years ago

Layer D — 1 million years ago

Layer C — 11 million years ago

Layer B — 28 million years ago

Layer A — 38 million years ago

Picture 3 shows what the horses probably looked like. The horse from 38 million years ago didn't look very much like horses of today. The horse from 28 million years ago looked more like the horses of today. Ⓥ The horse from 30 thousand years ago looked just like some horses that live today, but it was different from most of today's horses. Ⓦ ❀ 8 ERRORS ❀

LESSON 106

A

1	2	3	4
eohippus	front	light	**Vocabulary words**
itself	hoof	lighter	1. in danger
blast	member	bubble	2. open field
coach	hiding	family	3. herd
blasts			4. lighter

B   How Horses Changed Ⓐ

Picture 1 shows horse A. That horse lived 38 million years ago. Ⓑ Horse A is named eohippus. Ⓒ Eohippus is standing next to a horse of today. Next to the picture is a box that shows the front leg of eohippus next to the front leg of the horse that lives today. Ⓓ Name two ways that the front leg of eohippus is different from the front leg of a horse that lives today. Ⓔ

Picture 1

Horse A

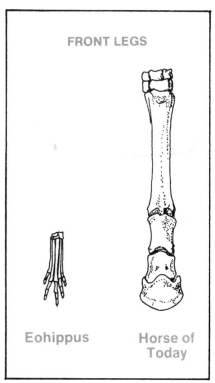

FRONT LEGS

Eohippus

Horse of Today

Eohippus did not stand on a hoof. Eohippus stood on toes. Ⓕ

Here are good questions. If eohippus does not look like a horse of today, how do we know that eohippus was a horse? How do we know that eohippus was not a member of the dog family? Ⓖ ❀ 2 ERRORS ❀

We know that eohippus is a member of the horse family because we have found skeletons of other horses that lived long ago. When we put

Textbook   Lesson 106   **213**

eohippus next to a horse that lives today, we see a very large change. But when we put eohippus next to a horse that lived 10 million years after eohippus, we do not see a large change. We see a small change. Ⓗ Look at picture 2. It shows the skeleton of eohippus next to the skeleton of the horse that lived 28 million years ago. A change has taken place. Ⓘ

Picture 2

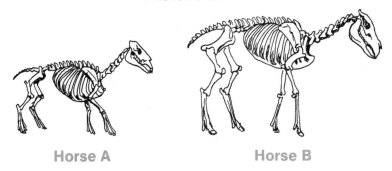

Horse A   Horse B

When we see the skeletons lined up, we can see just how the horse changed over millions of years. Look at picture 3. We know that eohippus is not a member of the dog family because we know that eohippus changed into a horse of today. Eohippus did not change into a dog. Ⓙ

Why did horses change? Here's the rule about the changes in the legs. **The changes in**

Picture 3

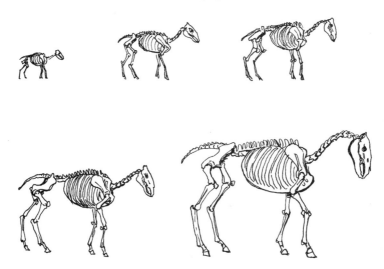

the legs made the horse faster. Ⓚ Eohippus was a hiding animal. It couldn't run as fast as a large cat like a lion. Eohippus stayed away from large cats. Ⓛ Eohippus ate grass and hid from danger. As millions of years went by, there was more food for animals like horses in the open fields. But an animal in the open had to run faster than eohippus. Ⓜ The horse that came after eohippus could run faster than eohippus. Ⓝ So the horse that came after eohippus could go out into the open more than eohippus did. Ⓞ If a large cat came near, the horse could run away.

The legs of early horses changed. The size of

the horses also changed. What happened to the size of the horses? Ⓟ Here's a rule about bigger animals. **Bigger animals are safer.** Ⓠ Why is a bigger animal safer? Ⓡ Bigger animals are safer because there aren't many animals that hunt big animals. But there are many animals that hunt small animals. An elephant is a very big animal. Ⓢ Not many animals hunt elephants. A rabbit is a very small animal. Ⓣ Many animals hunt rabbits. Ⓤ

When the horse was very small, many animals hunted it. When the horse got bigger, things changed. Ⓥ The bigger horse could go out into the open more than the smaller horse. Large cats hunted big horses, but if a large cat came along, the horse could take care of itself. Ⓦ But the bigger horse didn't have to worry about smaller cats or other smaller animals. Ⓧ

Here's the last rule about horses: **Animals are safer when they run together in a herd.** Ⓨ Wild horses run together in herds. Ⓩ

When the horse went into the open fields, the horse changed in three ways. It became bigger. It became faster. It ran in herds. Ⓐ

9 ERRORS

LESSON 107

1	2	3	4
heavy	crawl	figure	**Vocabulary words**
break	refrigerator	done	1. harm
idea	bubble	figured	2. rise
leaves	blasts	coach	3. ceiling
ready			4. lighter
bread			

B

Rules about Hot Air Ⓐ

You already know a rule about how hot air moves. Ⓑ

Look at the picture. It shows two hands and a fire. One of those hands will get burned if it doesn't move. The other hand will not get burned.

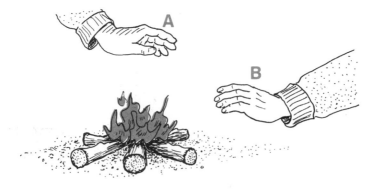

Which hand will get burned, hand A or hand B? Ⓒ

Which way does the heat move from the fire to reach hand A? Ⓓ

Here's the rule: **Hot air moves up.** Ⓔ

The fire makes the air hot. When the air gets hot, it moves. Which way does the hot air move? Ⓕ ✿ 2 ERRORS ✿

The hand that is above the fire gets burned because the hot air moves to that hand.

The hand that is next to the fire does not get burned.

If hot air moves up, hot air is lighter than cold air. Ⓖ

Let's say that you have two boxes. The boxes are the same size. One is filled with very cold air. One is filled with very hot air. Which box would be lighter? Ⓗ

The picture shows the boxes on a scale.

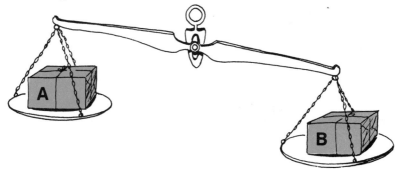

Which box is lighter—box A or box B? Ⓘ

Which box is filled with hotter air—box A or box B? Ⓙ

How do you know? Ⓚ

When hotter air is around colder air, the hotter air moves up like a bubble. Look at the picture of the balloon.

It is a hot air balloon. A fire heats the air inside the balloon.

When the air inside the balloon gets hotter,

which way does the balloon move?Ⓛ The
balloon moves up if the air inside the balloon is
hotter than the outside air.

If hotter air moves up, which way do you
think colder air moves?Ⓜ Cold air moves down.
The air inside a refrigerator is much colder than
the air outside the refrigerator. If we let the cold
air out of the refrigerator, which way will it
move?Ⓝ

Here's how you can show that the cold air
moves down. Lie down in front of a refrigerator
just after somebody has opened the refrigerator
door. When the door is open, the air inside the
refrigerator can move out of the refrigerator.
Which way will it move?Ⓞ

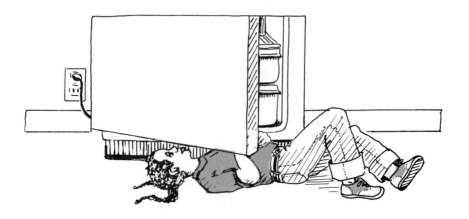

You will feel cold air falling on you.ⓟ

If you were in a hot air balloon, what would you have to do to make sure that the balloon kept moving up?ⓠ Let's say that you wanted the balloon to come down to the ground again. What would you do to the air?ⓡ

Why would the balloon move down when the air inside the balloon cooled off?ⓢ

Remember, hot air is like a bubble under water. It will move up. Cold air is like a stone in water. It will fall down. Hot air is light. Cold air is heavy.ⓣ

If you understand the rules about hot air, you know why smoke goes up.ⓤ

The rules about hot air also give you a clue about what to do if there is a fire. Some people stand up. Their head is in the smoke. There is far less smoke near the floor.ⓥ

The smart thing to do is to get down close to the floor. This is the part of the room that is the coolest. All the heat is going up. The heat is carrying the smoke with it. Close to the floor, the air is clearer, so you can see where you are going when you crawl from the room.ⓦ

❀ 8 ERRORS ❀

LESSON 108

A

1	2	3	4
Andrew Dexter	figured	enough	burst
Sidney Williams	ceiling	wrong	problem
magnetic	noticed	done	ready
research	evening	explained	careful
company			
address			

5	6
idea	**Vocabulary words**
fence	**1.** rake
breeze	**2.** rise
orange	**3.** harm

B

Sid Learns about Hot Air Ⓐ

Sid did not know which way hot air moves. Ⓑ One day his dad told him to rake the leaves in the yard. It was fall and the leaves had turned colors. Ⓒ There were red leaves and yellow leaves and orange leaves. The leaves fell from the trees every time a breeze blew. The trees still had lots of leaves on them, but they were pretty dry. If you rolled up one of the leaves in your hand, it would break into many small parts. **D** ✿ 2 ERRORS ✿

Sid's dad told him, "I would like you to keep the leaves in a pile near the back fence."

Sid said, "Dad, could I burn the leaves?"

"That's not a good idea," his dad said.

But Sid kept saying, "Please, dad. Could I burn them? Could I? Could I?" At last Sid's dad said, "All right. You can burn the leaves after

PICTURE 1

you rake them. But be very careful about where you make the fire." Ⓔ

"I'll be very careful," Sid said.

Sid raked the leaves very fast. Soon he had a large pile and he was ready to burn them.

Look at picture 2. Ⓕ Picture 2 shows Sid getting ready to start the fire. The picture shows that Sid is going to have a big problem when the fire starts. What is going to happen? Ⓖ

PICTURE 2

Sid started the fire and watched the flames get bigger and bigger. The fire made the air above it very hot. Which way did that air move?Ⓗ

And the hot air made the leaves in the tree hotter and hotter. Suddenly, the leaves in the tree burst into flames.

Sid jumped around yelling, "Fire! Fire!"

Sid's dad ran out and turned a hose on the fire. He put out the fire in the tree before it did much harm to the tree.Ⓘ Then Sid's father explained what Sid had done wrong.Ⓙ

Sid's dad explained that hot air rises.Ⓚ So if the fire is under the branch of a tree, the hot air will go right to that branch. If the air is hot enough, it will make the branch start to burn.

Later that evening, the air outside became very cold. Sid was sitting inside. He noticed that the air near the floor of the room was very cold.Ⓛ He noticed that the air closer to the ceiling of the room was different.Ⓜ Sid also noticed that there were flies in the room and all the flies were on the ceiling of the room. But Sid didn't know why.Ⓝ

Sid thought about the room. He figured out that the air coming into the room from outside was cold. He figured out which part of the room that cold air went to.Ⓞ He figured out that flies don't like cold air. So they go to the part of the room where the air is hot.Ⓟ

Then he figured out how he could make the room much warmer at the floor. Here's what he said to himself: "If you cut off the bottom part of the room, you'll cut off the part that gets cold."Ⓠ

Sid told his idea to his dad. His dad said, "Sid, that's not a very good idea." Then his dad explained why it isn't a good idea.Ⓡ ❄ 7 ERRORS ❄

LESSON 109

A

1	2	3
customer	Andrew Dexter	blasts
uniform	Sidney Williams	address
package	company	noticed
valuable	research	course
	magnetic	field

4	5	6
baseball	stack	strong-looking
shove	phone	important
basketball	loaf	counter
shoved	bread	favorite
playground	enough	

7
Vocabulary words
1. go out for a team
2. at bat
3. coach
4. daydream
5. stars
6. completely

Filling Out a Bank Form

Today's story will tell about banks. People keep money in banks.(A) When you put money in a bank, you must fill out a form.

Sid wants to keep his money in a bank. Before he can do that, he has to fill out the form that you see below.

Here are some facts about Sid.(B)

- His name is Sidney Williams.(C)
- His phone number is 345-1101.(D)
- He lives at 2233 Forest Street, San Francisco, California.(E)
- He is going to put $50 in the bank.(F)

1. Last Name _____ 2. First Name _____
3. Street Address _____
4. City _____ 5. State _____
6. Phone number _____
7. How much money are you putting in the bank? $ _____

C

Andrew Dexter Has Daydreams Ⓐ

Andrew Dexter worked in a bank. A bank is a place that holds money for people. Ⓑ If you have money and you want to keep it safe, you can take it to a bank. You go inside the bank and walk up to a counter. Ⓒ Behind the counter will be a person called a bank teller. Ⓓ You tell the bank teller that you would like to put your

money in the bank. The teller helps you fill out a form. Then the teller takes your money. When you want your money, you can go back to the bank and get it. ❀ 2 ERRORS ❀

Look at the picture on page 229. It shows a person leaving a bank. It shows a person standing at the counter giving money to a bank teller. Touch the person giving the money to the teller. Ⓔ Touch the teller. Ⓕ

The teller in the picture is Andrew Dexter. As you can see from the picture, Andrew Dexter was not a very strong-looking man. He was not very big. When you look at him in the picture, you would not believe that he became the strongest man who ever lived. But that is just what happened. Ⓖ

Of course, the picture shows Andrew before he became the strongest man who ever lived. When Andrew was a boy, he was not strong. There were many kids who could beat him up in a fight. Ⓗ

When Andrew went to high school, he went out for the baseball team. Ⓘ He wasn't good enough to stay on the team. Andrew went out for the football team. Ⓙ He wasn't big enough or fast enough or strong enough for the football team.Ⓚ Andrew went out for the basketball team. He wasn't tall enough or fast enough for that team either.Ⓛ

So Andrew did two things. He watched, and he did a lot of daydreaming.Ⓜ He watched all the games. He watched football games and baseball games. He watched games on TV and games at the playgrounds. He loved to watch.

*But he also dreamed. Everybody has dreams. Andrew's dreams were that he was a big star at football and baseball and basketball.Ⓝ When he was at work, he would dream. Here is one of his favorite dreams.Ⓞ

Andrew is watching a baseball game. Suddenly, the star player gets hurt. The crowd says, "Oh, no! We'll never win without our star player!"

The coach of the team looks around and sees Andrew. "Can you play?" the coach asks.

"Yes," Andrew says.

Andrew walks onto the field. The crowd says, "Who is that guy? He can't take the place of our star."* But then Andrew does things that are greater than anything anybody ever saw. He makes catches that the best star in the world can't make.

The crowd cheers. "That guy is great," they yell.

Then Andrew has a turn at bat. BLAM—he blasts the ball completely out of sight.

The crowd goes wild. "We love Andrew," they yell. "We love him. He's the greatest player in the world."

And Andrew becomes a star: a super, super, super star.℗

Andrew's dreams were just like the dreams that you have.Ⓠ In Andrew's dreams, people loved him. But Andrew's dreams were just dreams. In real life, not many people loved him. In fact, not many people noticed that he was around.Ⓡ

Get a picture of Andrew. There he was, working in the bank. He did his job, but his mind was often far from the bank.Ⓢ He dreamed about being important. He wanted to be the star. He wanted people to love him.Ⓣ

❀ 10 ERRORS ❀

LESSON 110

A

1	2	3	4
electricity	package	loaf	tingle
examine	research	phone	power
electromagnet	company	stack	tingled
	shoved	wrecking	oily
	bread	switch	tingling

5

Vocabulary words

1. customer
2. magnet
3. uniform
4. boss
5. valuable
6. magnetic

Learning about Checks

When you have money in a bank, you can write checks.Ⓐ Here's the rule about a check: **A check tells the bank how much money to pay somebody.**Ⓑ

If you write a check to Bill Jones for 10 dollars, the check tells the bank to pay Bill Jones 10 dollars.

If you write a check to Jan Smeed for 5 dollars, the check tells the bank to pay Jan Smeed 5 dollars.

Look at check A. Line 1 shows when the check was made out. When was it made out?Ⓒ

Check A

① March 15, 1980

② Pay to Tim Green   ③ 5 dollars

Five _____ dollars

④ Ann Bigg

Line 2 tells who the bank should pay. Who is that? Ⓓ

Line 3 tells how much money the bank should pay Tim Green. How much? Ⓔ

Line 4 tells who wrote the check. Who is that? Ⓕ

The bank is holding money for Ann Bigg. So the bank takes five dollars from Ann Bigg's money and pays it to Tim Green.

Look at check B.

Check B

May 20, 1979

Pay to <u>Sam Chin</u>   ⌐8 dollars

<u>Eight</u> ⎯⎯⎯⎯⎯⎯⎯⎯ dollars

Jim Brun

When was the check written? Ⓖ

Who should the bank pay? Ⓗ

How much should the bank pay? Ⓘ

Whose money does the bank use to pay Sam Chin? Ⓙ

C

Andrew Visits Magnetic Research Company Ⓐ

"Good morning," Andrew said to a customer. Ⓑ

The customer shoved a stack of checks toward Andrew. Andrew took care of the customer. "Thank you," Andrew said when he had finished. The customer didn't say one word to Andrew. Ⓒ The next customer was in front of Andrew, but Andrew's mind was moving from the bank. Ⓓ

Andrew is in a basketball uniform. Ⓔ The coach is saying to him, "I don't think I should let you play in this game because it's the most important game of the year. But our star player is hurt." Ⓕ

"I'll do a good job," Andrew says to the coach. ✿ 2 ERRORS ✿

Andrew is in the game now. There is almost no time left in the game. The other team is ahead by one basket. Ⓖ The ball comes to Andrew. He's too far from the basket, but he's got to take a chance at making a long shot. Time is running out. Ⓗ Andrew shoots and makes it. The crowd goes wild. "Who is that guy?" the fans ask.

"That's Andrew Dexter," somebody answers.

The other team passes the ball in.Ⓘ The clock is running down.Ⓙ Andrew leaps up and grabs the pass.Ⓚ Only four seconds are left in the game.Ⓛ Time for just one last shot. Andrew . . .Ⓜ

"Andrew, you have a customer."Ⓝ Andrew was suddenly back in the bank. Andrew's boss, Mr. Franks, was standing next to him.Ⓞ "Take care of your customer, Andrew," Mr. Franks said.Ⓟ

"Yes, Mr. Franks," Andrew said and smiled at the customer.

After finishing with the customer, Andrew noticed that the first customer had left a small package on the counter. Andrew picked up the package and brought it to Mr. Franks.

Mr. Franks made a phone call and then told Andrew, "I want you to take this package to Magnetic Research Company."Ⓠ Mr. Franks continued, "Magnetic Research Company is a very good customer of this bank, and this package is very valuable.Ⓡ So take the package over there right away.''

"Yes, sir," Andrew said. Andrew took the package, got in his old car, and began driving toward Magnetic Research Company. For a moment, Andrew wondered what was in the package. It wasn't any larger than a loaf of bread. But it was pretty heavy. What could it be?Ⓢ

Andrew has the basketball.(T) The ball almost slips from his hands. The crowd is counting down the seconds that are left in the game. "Four . . . three . . . two . . ." Andrew jumps up and shoots.(U) The ball slowly sails toward the basket. Then it slowly drops—right through the basket.

The sound of the crowd is so loud that the floor shakes. The fans are yelling, screaming, leaping from their seats.(V) People are lifting Andrew onto their shoulders. They are carrying him from . . .(W)

"Watch where you're driving," yelled the woman in the car next to Andrew's car. "Stay in your own lane."(X)

"Sorry," Andrew said softly. He told himself to pay attention to his driving.(Y)

✿ 9 ERRORS ✿

LESSON 111

A

1
leopard
African
chimpanzee

2
eyebrows
stopwatch
hang-time
airline
touchdown

3
tingled
wrecking
switch
tingling

4
power
scold
oily
scolded

5
teen-agers
streak
catcher
knock
electromagnets

6
Vocabulary words
1. electricity
2. motor
3. examine
4. steel
5. reason

B Andrew Is a Changed Person(A)

Twenty minutes after leaving the bank, Andrew was outside the Magnetic Research Company.(B) He was standing in front of a building that looked something like a school. There were many doors leading into the building. Andrew tried to open two of them, but they were locked. He walked around the building to a large steel door. It was in a part of the building that had no windows.(C) Andrew paused for a moment before trying the door.(D) He could hear a strange buzzing sound inside. He tugged on the door and it opened. He walked inside. And that is when it happened.(E)

❀ 2 ERRORS ❀

You know how magnets work.(F)Some things actually stick to magnets. If you have a strong magnet, you can pick up things like paper clips or nails.(G)

Here's something you may not know about magnets. You can use electricity to turn any steel bar into a magnet.(H) These magnets are called electromagnets.(I) They are used in automobile wrecking yards. Look at the picture.

It shows a large electromagnet picking up a car. Ⓙ If the person who is running the magnet wants to drop the car, the person just turns off the switch for the electricity. The electricity stops running through the electromagnet. And the electromagnet loses its power. Ⓚ

Why are we talking about magnets in the middle of the story about Andrew? Ⓛ We're talking about electromagnets because Andrew walked right into a room that was filled with electricity. Nobody knows exactly what happened or how it happened. We know that Andrew was holding the package. We also know what was in the package. It was a new motor that could pick up very small amounts of electricity from the air. These small amounts of electricity would run the motor. (M)

The Magnetic Research Company had planned to make car motors like the one in the package. These car motors wouldn't use gasoline. They would run on the electricity that is in the air. (N) The motor that was in the package was very small. It was a model of the bigger motors. (O) But the model worked. It ran by picking up very small amounts of electricity from the air.

There were very large amounts of electricity in the room where Andrew was standing. (P) When Andrew walked into the room, the motor began to work so fast that it actually melted. It burned Andrew's hands. But it did more than that. It put millions of kilograms of power into Andrew's body. Of course he didn't know it. In fact, he didn't know exactly what happened. He had opened the steel door and walked into a large dark room. A loud, strange noise made him feel very dizzy. The noise got louder and louder. He could hear somebody's voice saying, "You can't come in here. We're . . ." Then he noticed that his hands felt like they were on fire.Ⓠ He tried to drop the package, but he couldn't. It was stuck to his hands.

Suddenly, the noise stopped. Lights came on. Three men and a woman were in front of Andrew. The woman was saying to one of the men, "Wasn't that door locked? I told Jimmy that we were going to run a test."

One man was saying to Andrew, "Are you all right? You don't look well."

Andrew didn't feel well. His hands hurt, but he couldn't let go of the package. One of the men said, "Let me take that." He grabbed the package and jumped back. "Wow," he said. "Did I ever get a shock."Ⓡ

The man touched the package again. This time he didn't get a shock. He pulled Andrew's fingers from the package. Then he opened the package. "Oh no," he said. "Look at it. It's completely wrecked."

The woman shook her head. "Two years. It took us two years to make that machine. And look at it now." Ⓢ

Before Andrew left the building, a doctor examined him. Ⓣ The doctor put some oily stuff on Andrew's hands. He asked, "How do you feel?"

Andrew said, "I'm all right," but he felt very strange. His hands and arms tingled. Ⓤ His legs tingled. Even his eyes had a kind of tingling feeling. "I'm all right," he repeated.

But Andrew was not the same person that he had been. Andrew started to find out just how different he was when he left the Magnetic Research Company. His car door was stuck. So he gave it a tug. He pulled the door completely off the car. Ⓥ ❀ 13 ERRORS ❀

LESSON 112

A

1
professional
Titans
league
pardon
whistle

2
Denny Brock
scolded
eyebrows
knock
African

3
catcher
teen-agers
leopard
streak

4
tackle
worth
chimpanzee
tackles

5
stopwatch
touchdown
hang-time
airline

6
trunk
full-grown
easily
million
sorry

7
Vocabulary words
1. home run
2. first base
3. groceries
4. follow
5. fired
6. reason

The Strength of Animals

The story that you will read today tells about the strength of humans. Humans are very weak when we compare humans with some other animals.Ⓐ Picture 1 shows a leopard. The leopard may weigh only 45 kilograms. Yet a leopard can carry an animal that weighs 70 kilograms while the leopard climbs a tree.Ⓑ The leopard would look as if it is carrying something that weighs only a few kilograms.Ⓒ

PICTURE 1

A lion is much stronger than a leopard. People have seen this: A large lion carries an animal that weighs about 90 kilograms. The lion then jumps a fence that is over 2 meters high. Ⓓ Picture 2 shows a large lion. Ⓔ

PICTURE 2

Chimpanzees are very strong. If a strong man pulls down on a rope as hard as he can pull, he may pull with a force of over 90 kilograms. A chimpanzee can pull with a force of over 220 kilograms.Ⓕ And a chimpanzee weighs only about 45 kilograms. Picture 3 shows a chimpanzee.Ⓖ

PICTURE 3

The strongest land animal is the elephant, and the strongest elephant is the African elephant. Ⓗ An African elephant can pick up a horse as easily as you would pick up a baby. It can lift logs that 30 men could not lift. It can tear trees out of the ground. It can knock down buildings or tip a large truck over. Look at what the elephant in picture 4 is doing. Ⓘ

PICTURE 4

C

Andrew Gets Fired Ⓐ

Andrew felt silly driving back to the bank in a car that had no door. Ⓑ The door was in the trunk of the car. People looked at Andrew and smiled. "What a nut," he heard one driver say. Ⓒ But Andrew still didn't feel right, and he still didn't know that he was just about as strong as a full-grown African elephant. Ⓓ An elephant can walk right through a brick wall just as easily as you would walk through a wall made of paper. An elephant can lift a quarter horse just as easily as you could pick up a bag of groceries. Ⓔ   ❋ 2 ERRORS ❋

When Andrew walked inside the bank, Mr. Franks walked up to him. Andrew could tell that Mr. Franks was not happy. When Mr. Franks was mad at somebody, he would make his eyebrows come together and he would stare at the person. That's just what he was doing now. Ⓕ

"Andrew," he said. "I would like to talk with you. Follow me." So Andrew followed. Mr. Franks led the way to a small room in the back of the bank. Mr. Franks told Andrew,

"You don't think about what you are doing. Why didn't you ring the bell by the front door at Magnetic Research Company instead of going in a side door?" Ⓖ

"Well, I didn't see a bell," Andrew said.

"That's your problem. You don't see. You don't think. Your mind is always a million miles away. Ⓗ The people at Magnetic Research Company are very, very unhappy. And so am I." Mr. Franks scolded Andrew for a few more minutes. Ⓘ Then he told Andrew, "I'm very sorry, but you can't work here anymore. You're fired." Ⓙ

Andrew didn't feel bad when he heard this announcement. He still felt a little strange. Ⓚ "All right," he said, and went back to his teller window to get his coat.

Then he went out for a walk. He walked to a playground. A bunch of teen-agers were playing baseball. When Andrew was just outside the fence, one of the boys hit a home run. The ball sailed over the fence. It was just about three meters over Andrew's head. But for some strange reason, Andrew jumped up to catch the ball. Nobody had ever seen a person jump three meters high because nobody had ever jumped three meters high before Andrew did it. He jumped up, and up, and up. He reached out, and . . . he caught it. Ⓛ

The boys stopped playing. The boy who had hit the ball was not running toward first base. He was standing and staring at Andrew.

His eyes were very big.Ⓜ The other boys who had been watching the ball were now watching Andrew. Their eyes were very big.

Andrew smiled. He jumped again and threw the ball to the catcher. The ball went through the air like a streak.Ⓝ The ball moved over 200 kilometers per hour. When the ball hit the catcher's mitt, it made a sound—WHAP—that you could hear nearly a kilometer away.Ⓞ The catcher fell over backwards.Ⓟ The catcher shook his mitt from his hand and ran around shaking his hands and blowing on them.Ⓠ

❋ 8 ERRORS ❋

LESSON 113

A

1	**2**	**3**
interrupt	Denny Brock	blamed
Charlie	Titans	whistles
champion	tackles	pardon
	worth	touchdown

4

Vocabulary words

1. show up

2. professional football league

3. blame

4. deaf

B

Learning about Football

You're going to read about a football team.
So you have to know some things about football
games.

The picture below shows the things the player must wear. These things are part of the football uniform. Ⓐ

This is a helmet. Ⓑ

These are shoulder pads. Ⓒ

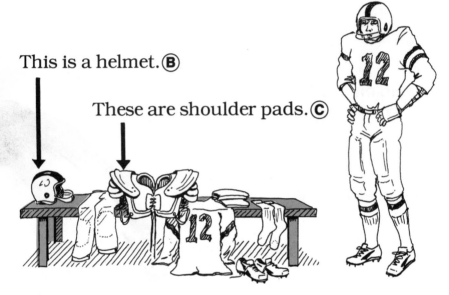

Here are facts about the game of football:
- Football is played with 11 players on a team. Ⓓ
- Two teams play.
- The field is about 90 meters long. Ⓔ
- The team that has the ball tries to move the ball to the goal line at the other end of the field. Ⓕ
- If the team gets all the way to the other end of the field, the team scores a **touchdown.** That is worth 6 points. Ⓖ

- To move down the field, the team runs with the ball or passes the ball. **Ⓗ**
- The other team tries to stop the team that has the ball. This team tackles players who have the ball and tries to catch any passes. **Ⓘ**
- Each team has kickers. The kicker kicks the ball after each touchdown. The kicker also kicks the ball if a team is stopped and has to turn the ball over to the other team. **Ⓙ**

The picture below shows the black team running with the ball. The white team is trying to tackle the player with the ball. **Ⓚ**

C

Andrew Meets Denny Brock Ⓐ

Andrew was standing outside the playground fence. He was smiling.Ⓑ The boys walked over to the fence. They were smiling. "Hey, man," one of them said. "What's your name?"

Andrew told them.Ⓒ

Another boy asked, "Are you a baseball star?"Ⓓ

"No," Andrew said. He was going to say, "I work in the bank," but then he remembered that he had been fired. "No," he repeated. "I'm looking for a job."

"Wow," one boy said. "You should get a job playing baseball. I have never seen anybody throw or catch the way you do." ❊ 2 ERRORS ❊

Andrew talked to the boys for a few minutes. Then he said goodbye and walked away from the playground. His mind was still dizzy.Ⓔ What had happened? He had just done two things that are impossible. Yet he did them.Ⓕ He—Andrew Dexter—had just caught a ball that nobody could catch, and he had just thrown it the way nobody could throw it. Wow, it really happened. It really, really happened. Ⓖ

• • •

Denny Brock was mad. Denny Brock was almost always mad. He was the coach of the worst team in the Professional Football League, the Titans. Ⓗ Last year, his team had won one game. Ⓘ The year before that, his team had not won a single game. Ⓙ Denny's players were unhappy. Ⓚ They blamed each other. Ⓛ The players blamed the coaches. They blamed the rain or the snow or anything else they could blame. The people who owned the team were as unhappy as the players. At least once a week they would remind Denny, "We pay a lot of money for good football players. We should have a good team. But we don't. And if the team doesn't get any better, we'll have to fire you." Ⓜ

The players and the owners were not the only people who were unhappy. The fans were unhappy, too. When most teams in the Professional Football League play, more than 50 thousand fans come to the ball park and watch the game. When the Titans played, less than 15 thousand people showed up. **(N)** The team didn't have many fans, so the team didn't make money, so the players didn't get paid as much as they wanted, so the players were unhappy, so they didn't play well, so the owners were unhappy. **(O)**

If you understand the kind of problems that Denny had every day, you can see why he was mad most of the time. You can also see why he wasn't very happy when Andrew came to the ball park of the Titans and tried to talk to Denny. **(P)** The team was on the field trying to practice some running plays. **(Q)** The coaches were doing as much running as the players. **(R)** The coaches were blowing whistles and trying to tell the players how to run the play the right way. Denny was standing on the sidelines, with his arms folded. **(S)** Every now and then, Denny would yell, "No, you clowns. Use your head and think about what you're doing." **(T)** Then Denny would mumble something like, "I think they're daydreaming half the time." **(U)**

"Pardon me," Andrew said. "I would like to try out for your team." **(V)**

Andrew was standing behind Denny.

Andrew had told a guard at the gate that he had
a meeting with Denny.  That wasn't true, but
it was the only way that Andrew could think of
to meet Denny.

Denny turned around and gave Andrew a mean look. "Who let you in here?" he demanded.(X)

"I told a guard that I had a meeting with you so—"

"That jerk," Denny said.(Y) "That dumb guard should know better than that. Now get out of here. We're having a practice."(Z)

"I can help your team," Andrew said. "I'm very good at—"(A)

"Are you deaf?" Denny yelled. "I said get out of here."

"But I can help your . . ."(B)

"Listen, buddy, get out of here or I'll have you thrown out."(C) 🌸 11 ERRORS 🌸

LESSON 114

A

1	2	3	4
chitter	treat	coaches	pretended
Charlie	stopwatch	breath	uneasy
interrupted	hang-time	muscle	becoming
chittering	champion	couple	sweat
	treating	believe	laughter

5

Vocabulary words

interrupt

B   Seconds

The story that you will read today tells
about seconds.Ⓐ A second is a unit of time. It is
not a very long unit of time. If you count slowly,
one . . . two . . . three . . . four . . . , you're
counting seconds.Ⓑ

Find a clock or a watch with a second hand.
Count the seconds. Remember to count each
time the second hand crosses a dot.Ⓒ

A stopwatch is used to measure seconds. **D** A stopwatch starts with the second hand pointing straight up. Each time one second passes, the second hand moves one dot this way: **E**

Touch stopwatch A.Ⓕ Stopwatch A shows that no seconds have passed.

Which stopwatch shows that 3 seconds have passed?Ⓖ

Which stopwatch shows that 4 seconds have passed?Ⓗ

Which stopwatch shows that 6 seconds have passed?Ⓘ

Which stopwatch shows that 7 seconds have passed?Ⓙ

C

The Titans Make Fun of AndrewⒶ

Andrew was trying to get a job with the Titans.Ⓑ Denny Brock wouldn't listen to Andrew. Just then, one of the coaches who worked for Denny ran up. "Denny," he said. He was out of breath. "You're not going to believe this, but Charlie just pulled a leg muscle.Ⓒ It looks bad, and I don't think he'll be able to kick the ball for a couple of weeks. The doc is looking at him now and maybe he'll be all right, but—" **D**

"The only good player we have on this team," Denny shouted. "And he pulls his leg muscle. I don't believe this. I just don't believe it." ❀ 2 ERRORS ❀

Denny kicked a helmet that was on the field next to him. He hurt his toe and hopped around. **E**

"I can kick," Andrew said. "I think I can kick as far as anybody." **F**

*Denny was still hopping. "You can kick as far as anybody. Did you hear that, Joe?" Denny pretended to laugh. **G** "This guy walks in off the street and tells us he can kick as far as anybody. All right, smart guy. What's the hang-time on your best kick?" **H**

"I really . . . I don't know."

Denny said, "Here he is, Joe. A guy who can kick as well as anybody, but he doesn't know what his hang-time is. I'm not even sure he knows what hang-time means. Do you, buddy? What is hang-time?"

"Well, the hang-time . . ." Andrew knew

what hang-time was. He'd* watched a lot of games. But Denny was making him uneasy.Ⓘ "The hang-time . . ."

Denny interrupted. "It's how long the ball stays in the air. That's what hang-time is. Now get out of here."Ⓙ

Andrew was becoming angry. "I can kick the ball as well as anybody," he said loudly. "I can do it," Andrew yelled. He ran onto the playing field and picked up a football. One of the players called to Denny, "You want me to throw him out?"Ⓚ

"No, don't throw him out until he shows us how well he can kick," Denny shouted. "He tells us he can kick the ball as well as anybody. Of course, he doesn't know what his best hang-time is. And of course nobody knows who this guy is. But he just happens to be as good as any kicker in professional football."Ⓛ

The players started to laugh.Ⓜ Some of the players took off their helmets and wiped the sweat from their faces.Ⓝ Soon, all the players and the coaches were watching Andrew. He was standing in the middle of the field holding a football and feeling very silly. "Where do you want me to kick it?'' Andrew asked.

The players and the coaches laughed. ''Up,'' Denny shouted, and pointed up. ''I want to see a four-second hang-time.''◉ Everybody was laughing.

A couple of the players pointed up. ''That's it, man,'' one player yelled. ''Just put that ball up there long enough for us to run down the field and catch it.''

The laughter continued and Andrew tried not to listen to it. It bothered him, though. "Think about what you're doing," he told himself.Ⓟ He held the ball in front of him. He heard a couple of the players yelling, "Look at that. He's holding the ball all wrong." They laughed louder.Ⓠ ❁ 9 ERRORS ❁

LESSON 115

1	**2**	**3**
sidelines	argue	earn
upright	treating	scratch
Wildcats	argues	paid
championship	chittering	scratched
	argued	

4

Vocabulary words

1. slight
2. stands
3. time

B

Andrew Kicks Ⓐ

Everybody was laughing at Andrew, but he tried not to think about it. He thought about kicking the ball.Ⓑ Andrew dropped the ball and kicked it as hard as he could with his right foot. CRACK. The sound of his foot hitting the ball was so loud it sounded like a gunshot. "Crack, Crack, Crack," it echoed around the stands. The ball went almost straight up. It moved so fast that some of the players didn't even see it leave Andrew's foot. Within a second, it was a small speck, hundreds of meters overhead. Ⓒ If you looked very hard, you could see the ball. "Rack, rack," the sound was still echoing around the stands. Ⓓ ❄ 2 ERRORS ❄

Then there was silence. You could hear a slight breeze and the flapping of the flag at the far end of the playing field. Ⓔ There was the sound of a bird chittering in the stands. Ⓕ In the distance was the sound of a bus and a few car horns. But there was not one sound from Denny, not one sound from the football players or from the other coaches. Not a word.Ⓖ They stood there staring straight up into the sky. And they stood there and they stood there and they watched and they waited. Finally, the ball seemed to get bigger and bigger.Ⓗ Now you could see that it was coming down very fast. It didn't land in the field. It landed in one of the stands. BLAM.Ⓘ Then the ball bounced up twenty meters. Again it came down and bounced and finally rolled to a stop.

The first person to talk was one of the players. "I don't believe this," he yelled. "This is amazing." Then other players began to yell. "Do it again," one yelled. "Yeah, man, once more."

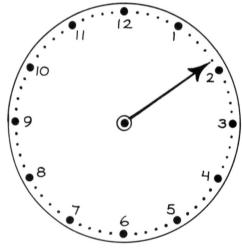

The coach standing next to Denny held out a stopwatch. The coach explained to Denny. "I timed his hang-time. You probably saw that it was more than four seconds."

Denny looked at the stopwatch. His eyes became very large.Ⓙ Yes, Andrew's hang-time was more than four seconds. It was more than five seconds and more than six seconds. The picture shows what his hang-time was.Ⓚ

The players were crowding around Andrew now. "What's your secret?" one asked. "Is it the funny way you hold the ball before you kick?"

"Get out of the way," another player said. "I want to see him do it again." The player handed Andrew a ball. "Do it again, man," the player said.

So Andrew did. It was a better kick than the first one. The noise of his foot hitting the ball was so loud that a couple of players put their hands over their ears. The ball went up, up, almost out of sight.Ⓛ Then down, down it came, this time landing about 30 meters away, right in the middle of the field. All the players looked at the coaches' stopwatches to see what the hang-time was.Ⓜ

"Come on," one of the players said. "This isn't happening. Nobody can kick a ball with a hang-time of 11 seconds." **(N)** That player was almost right. There was only one person who could kick a ball with a hang-time of 11 seconds. **(O)**

"Okay, you guys," Denny shouted to his football players. "Get back to your practice." Denny blew three short blasts on his whistle. "Now," he shouted. **(P)**

Slowly, the players put on their helmets and trotted away from Andrew. Before leaving, some of them slapped him on the back. "Good kicking, man," they said.

"Thanks," Andrew replied. He felt very strange. The other players were treating him like a star.

"Let's talk," Denny said, putting his arm around Andrew's shoulder. **(Q)** "Let's go have a soft drink and do a little talking." Denny's voice was not mean. It was very friendly. He was being nice to Andrew because he wanted Andrew to play for the Titans. **(R)** ❋ 11 ERRORS ❋

LESSON 116

1	**2**	**3**
allow	championship	mistake
referee	earn	scratched
elbow	sidelines	argues
ruin	paid	mistakes
bury		

4	**5**
upright	**Vocabulary words**
fumble	**1.** kid around
Wildcats	**2.** mention
airline	**3.** argue
fumbled	**4.** worth
	5. offer

B   ## Professional Football Players

Some football players play football for fun.
But the best players play professional football.
For these players, playing football is their
job. Ⓐ These players make money playing
football. The work is very hard because only the

best players play professional football. So if you are a professional football player, you play against the best players there are. These players tackle very hard and run very fast.

Professional football players earn a lot of money. A player who is very good at running with the ball may earn over 200 thousand dollars a year.ⓑ Most players do not earn that much. Some players make only 50 thousand dollars a year. But 50 thousand dollars a year is a lot of money. It is more money than a teacher earns. It is more money than a flight attendant earns. It is more money than a bank teller earns. Airline pilots earn more than 50 thousand dollars a year. So do most doctors.ⓒ

The football players that are worth the most money are the players the football fans want to see.ⓓ If fans go to a game just so they can see one player, that player is worth a lot of money.

Denny Gives Andrew a Job Ⓐ

The two men walked over to a bench on the sidelines. Ⓑ "Joe," Denny yelled in a mean voice. "Have one of the boys bring us some soft drinks." Ⓒ

Denny mentioned how nice the weather had been. Ⓓ Then Denny said, "Okay, I don't know how you do that kicking, but we want you. You have to remember that kicking out there in an empty field is a lot different from kicking in a game when four monsters are coming after you like trucks. I mean, we'll have to work with you and teach you a lot. But we want you to play for the Titans."(E) 🌸 2 ERRORS 🌸

"Okay," Andrew said, and smiled.

Denny didn't jump up and down with joy. He thought that Andrew was trying to play a joke on him. Players don't just say, "Okay, I'll be on your team." Here's what almost every player says: "How much do I get paid?" Then Denny offers a small amount of money and the player argues for more money. And they argue and argue.(F)

Denny had been ready to argue with Andrew. Denny knew that fans would come from all over to see somebody kick the ball hundreds of meters into the air. Even if the Titans lost, people would pay money just to see Andrew kick the ball. Here's what Denny was thinking: If the team had Andrew, at least 10 thousand more fans would come to each game.(G) So the team would make at least 50 thousand dollars each game if Andrew played.(H) The team could probably make another 50 thousand dollars by letting the games go on TV. So Andrew was worth at least 100 thousand dollars for each game that he played. Ⓘ Denny was ready to pay Andrew a lot of money—a lot of money. But when Denny had asked Andrew to play for the Titans, Andrew didn't argue about money. Denny didn't know what to say.

Denny looked at Andrew. Then he said, "Well—I don't even know your name." Andrew told him, and the men shook hands. Then Denny continued, "Well, how much money do you think you should get?" Ⓙ

Andrew scratched his cheek and made a face. Ⓚ "I think I should make at least as much as I made at my last job."

"Tell me how much and I'll tell you if we can do it."

"A thousand dollars a month," Andrew said. Ⓛ

First Denny smiled, and then he shook his head. Then he smiled again. Then he made a face. Ⓜ Then he said, "Come on, now. I don't know if you're kidding around with me or what you're doing. No player of mine is going to work for only a thousand dollars a month. I'll pay you ten thousand dollars a month. That's 120 thousand dollars a year." **(N)**

Andrew had seen a lot of money when he worked in the bank. He had counted piles of money worth more than ten thousand dollars, but he never thought that he would earn ten thousand dollars a month. "That's great," Andrew said, smiling. "That's really great."

The men shook hands again. Denny was very happy because he didn't pay Andrew very much. **(O)** Andrew was very happy because he was going to make more money than he ever thought he'd make. **(P)** 🌀 9 ERRORS 🌀

LESSON 117

1	2	3
newspapers	fumbled	ruin
whenever	referee	bury
loud-speaker	Wildcats	elbow
airline	mistakes	buried
		ruining

4	5	6
announcements	simply	**Vocabulary words**
secret	talents	1. field goal
impression	famous	2. holler
respond	reporters	3. touchdown
reply	uneasy	4. roars
		5. allow

B

Andrew Plays in His First Game Ⓐ

Before Andrew's first game, many announcements appeared in the newspapers. These announcements told about the Titans' secret new player. Ⓑ The announcements gave the impression that the Titans had a player who could turn the Titans into a winning team. Ⓒ Through these announcements, the Titans hoped to bring more people to the game. Here's what one announcement said: Ⓓ

> "Coach Denny Brock did not respond when he was asked what his new star player could do. He simply smiled and said, 'Andrew Dexter has some talents that nobody has seen on a football field before.' " Ⓔ 🌸 2 ERRORS 🌸

Before Andrew's first game, he was already famous. He talked to reporters from TV stations and from newspapers. But he didn't tell them what he could do for the team. Whenever a reporter asked about what he would do in the game, he would reply "All I can tell you is this: I can do my part of the game better than anybody else in the world." Ⓕ

● ● ●

For the first time in four years, the stands were filled with people. Ⓖ Most of the fans were talking about Andrew Dexter. You could hear them talking near the hot dog stand.(H)

"He doesn't look like much," one fan would say.(I)

"Yes," another would say, "this had better not be a trick to get us out here."

But the fans did come to see Andrew. Over fifty thousand fans crowded into the stands.(J) None of the fans really thought that the Titans would win this game, because the Titans were playing the best team in the league—the Wildcats.(K) The sun was bright, and a slight breeze was blowing.(L) The air was just cold enough so you could see your breath. Most of the fans wore heavy shoes and mittens.(M)

Now came the time when all players start to feel a little uneasy. Just before the game, they know that they will go out on the field. Everybody will be watching them. Will they do well? Will they make mistakes? These questions run through the players' minds.(N) Sometimes the players have daydreams of being a star who wins the game. But there are very few stars on a team. Most of the players must do their job so the stars can look like stars.(O)

The name of each player was announced

over the loud-speaker. Each player ran onto the playing field, and the crowd whooped and hollered. They whooped very loudly for Andrew. Now the players on the field were ready. They felt like they couldn't catch their breath. Ⓟ They felt a little exhausted although they hadn't started to play yet.

The teams lined up. The Titans were ready to kick to the Wildcats. Andrew was more frightened than the other players. He had never played in front of a huge crowd. One of the other Titans held the ball. Andrew ran up and kicked it. BOOOOM. Ⓠ

The crowd roared as the ball went up, up, up, up. Everybody in the stands was standing, looking straight up into the blue sky at a tiny speck. Ⓡ The ball came down, down, down. But it wasn't caught by a member of the other team. Ⓢ The ball stayed in the air so long that the Titans ran all the way down the field before it came down. And the ball was caught by a Titan. The Titans had the ball only ten meters from the goal line. Ⓣ

As Andrew left the field, the people in the stands were yelling and cheering. Ⓤ The players

from the Wildcats were arguing that the Titans should not be allowed to have the ball. Ⓥ The Wildcats insisted that the kick was unfair. But the referee didn't take the ball from the Titans. Ⓦ So the Titans ran three plays and scored a touchdown. Ⓧ

The Titans kicked off again. BOOOOM. This time, the ball floated all the way past the end of the field, and the Wildcats had the ball. Ⓨ The Wildcats moved down the field, passing the ball and running the ball. Then, on one play, a runner fumbled the ball and a player from the Titans fell on it. Ⓩ The Titans had the ball.

The Titans ran two plays and lost over fifteen meters. Ⓐ They ran another play and lost another four meters. The crowd started to boo the Titans. Ⓑ The team was now eighty meters from a touchdown. Andrew came onto the field. The announcer said, "It looks as if the Titans are going to try to kick a field goal—an eighty-meter field goal." Ⓒ The people in the stands didn't laugh, because they had seen how high Andrew could kick the ball. Ⓓ ✷ 13 ERRORS ✷

LESSON 118

A

1	2	3
frequently	Handy Andy	ruining
towel	elbow	bury
	upright	awful
	ka-splat	buried
	cracked	kicked

4	5	6
whooped	laughed	**Vocabulary words**
slapped	crowded	1. knocked out
plowed	echoed	2. pat
waited	bounced	3. trot
pushed	approached	4. ruin
		5. charge
		6. tackle

B Andrew Meets Smiling Sam Ⓐ

The Titans had the ball eighty meters away from a score. Ⓑ Andrew was going to try an eighty-meter field goal. No fan had ever seen a field goal that long. They had seen fifty-meter field goals when the wind was blowing in the same direction as the kick. But the wind was blowing against the kick today.Ⓒ

The fans were quiet. The players on the Wildcats were jumping around, yelling things at the Titans. "Come on, you bums," they yelled. "What's that tiny foot going to try to do? You'll never make it, jelly face."Ⓓ ❊ 2 ERRORS ❊

The ball came back. A Titan held it in place and Andrew kicked it. The crowd whooped. The ball sailed 180 meters and went completely out of the ball park. But it did not pass between the upright poles. So it was not a field goal.Ⓔ

Some of the Titan players patted Andrew on the back. "Good try," they said, and Andrew felt a little better.Ⓕ The biggest player on the team, Mean George, said, "You'll get it next time. Just stay cool."Ⓖ

The Wildcats scored a touchdown and the game was tied—7 to 7.Ⓗ Then the Wildcats scored another touchdown. The score was now 14 to 7.Ⓘ And the Wildcats were just running over the Titans.Ⓙ Two Titans were hurt and had to leave the game. The player that was hurting them was Smiling Sam.Ⓚ He was one of the biggest Wildcats. Three of his front teeth

were missing, and he smiled. It wasn't a friendly smile, though. It was a very mean smile. Ⓛ "Going to get you guys," Smiling Sam would say to the Titans. Then he would fly into one of them with his helmet down and his legs pushing his huge body as fast as it could go.

Andrew was standing on the sidelines watching Smiling Sam. "He's playing dirty," Andrew said to one of the coaches. "He just hit one of our guys with his elbow." **Ⓜ**

"Yeah," the coach said. "He's a mean one."

"Well, we should make him stop doing that."

"How could we stop him?" the coach asked. "We would need a truck to stop that animal."

"I'll tell him to stop," Andrew said.

"Hey, Andrew," the coach said. "We need you in one piece. Just stay away from that guy." **Ⓝ**

The Titans had the ball. The Wildcats pushed them back on three running plays. **Ⓞ** It was time for Andrew to go out and kick the ball. He trotted out on the field. **Ⓟ** Andrew ran up to Smiling Sam. He looked up at him and said, "Listen, you stop playing dirty. Football is a good game, but you're ruining it. So cut it out." **Ⓠ**

Smiling Sam gave Andrew a big smile, a very big one. Then, while he was still smiling, he said, "I'm going to get you, you little creep." Ⓡ

"Don't try it," Andrew said. "I'll knock you out of the game."

The Wildcats laughed. Some Wildcats slapped Smiling Sam on the back, and Smiling Sam didn't take his eyes off Andrew. The teams lined up for the kick. The ball came to Andrew. But Andrew didn't try to kick it. He just put it under one arm and waited. Ⓢ Smiling Sam plowed through the Titans and charged at Andrew as hard as he could. Andrew could hear him yelling, "I got you now."

Just as Smiling Sam was ready to bury his helmet in Andrew's chest, Andrew put his head down and charged. KA-SPLAT. A terrible sound, almost like a clap of thunder, echoed through the stands as the players hit head-on. Ⓣ Smiling Sam flew backwards into two of his own players. He knocked them about five meters back. He was knocked out. His helmet was cracked. And two of his teeth were loose. Ⓤ

Andrew ran forward. Two more Wildcats tried to tackle him. They bounced off. He ran down the field. The fans were cheering and yelling and stamping as he approached the goal line. A touchdown. The score was tied. Ⓥ

Titan players crowded around Andrew. "Wow," one of them said. "You're the greatest."

"Yeah," another one said. "I didn't know you could run with the ball." Ⓦ

Andrew ran with the ball three more times during that game and he made three more touchdowns. The Titans won the game, 35 to 21. Ⓧ ❀ 12 ERRORS ❀

LESSON 119

1	2	3
Handy Andy	reporters	noticed
firing	themselves	realized
towel	members	dressed
newspapers	holler	squeezed
practices	chances	frightened

4

Vocabulary words

1. awful
2. frequently
3. championship
4. packed

B

Andrew Begins to Change Ⓐ

The newspapers were filled with stories about Andrew. They called him "Handy Andy, the man who does it all for the Titans." Ⓑ Andrew was very busy. He had to go to the practices. He also had to talk to reporters. And when he left the practice field every day, a group of fans would be outside. They wanted him to sign his name in their books.Ⓒ

Andrew didn't daydream anymore. His life was like a great daydream so he didn't have time for anything except living.Ⓓ He worked very hard. And the other members of the Titans started to work hard too. They started to become proud of themselves and proud of their team. ❋ 2 ERRORS ❋

Before Andrew had come around, people would say to the other players, "Oh, you play for that awful team, the Titans."Ⓔ Now the people would say, "Wow, you play with the Titans. They are the hottest team in football."Ⓕ The players wanted to show the fans that the team wasn't just a one-man team. They wanted to show that there were 11 good football players on the field when the Titans played.Ⓖ

When the players played better, the coaches didn't yell as much. Before Andrew came along, you would never hear Denny say, "Good job." But now, he would frequently holler to his players, "That's the way to run that play. Good job."Ⓗ

And the people who owned the Titans

didn't tell Denny that they were thinking of firing him. Instead, they asked things like this: "What do you think our chances are for winning the championship?" Ⓘ

Denny would reply, "Our chances of winning the championship are pretty good if we keep playing the way we're playing."

And the fans were happy. The people who lived in Andrew's city felt that the team was their team. They talked about the team. People who didn't know each other would talk on the bus or in the grocery store. "Did you see Handy Andy and the Titans last Sunday?" they would say. Then they would start talking about the game. Ⓙ

Every Sunday the stands were packed. There were no empty seats. And when the Titans came onto the field, the fans would cheer. The fans would think "That's my team and it's the best team there is. Yea for the Titans."

For five Sundays it was the same. Andrew would come onto the field when the team couldn't move. He would either kick the ball or run with it. When he kicked, he would usually make a field goal. When he ran with it he would always make a touchdown. (K) Nobody could stop him. Sometimes three or four players would hit him at the same time. For those players, running into Andrew was just like running into the side of a truck. They bounced back and Andrew kept going.

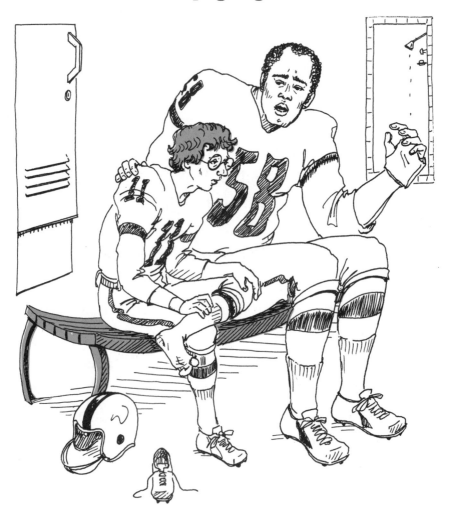

*But then on the sixth Sunday, Andrew felt strange. When he was getting dressed for the game, he noticed that his hands and feet were tingling. Ⓛ He had the same feeling that he had felt earlier at Magnetic Research Company when he had walked into the room filled with electricity.

Now he was sitting on the bench in front of his locker putting his shoes on. Suddenly, he realized what was wrong. He grabbed the locker handle and squeezed it as hard as he could. Ⓜ Instead of bending it like a piece of clay, he put a tiny dent in* it. Ⓝ He tried again. The outcome was the same. Ⓞ Andrew Dexter was losing his super strength.

He was still strong, perhaps as strong as a quarter horse, which meant that he was probably as strong as five or six very strong men. Ⓟ But he didn't have the strength of an African elephant anymore.

He was frightened. If he was getting weaker and weaker, he would soon lose all his super strength. He would just be plain old Andrew Dexter again. Mean George walked by the bench and slapped Andrew on the back. "Big game today," Mean George said. "You're going to do it for us again today." Ⓠ

"George," Andrew said, looking up at the huge man. "I . . . I don't think I'm going to be . . . I don't . . ." Ⓡ

"What's the matter, man?" George said and sat next to Andrew. The bench bent down under the weight of Mean George. Ⓢ "Andy, you look sick."

Andrew said, "You guys are going to have to help me out. I don't think I'll be able to run or kick as well today."

"You got to," George said. "Without you, we're just a bunch of bums."

"No," Andrew shouted. "Don't you say that. You guys are great. You just don't know it. You can do it without me. You just have to tell yourselves that you can." Ⓣ ❋ 14 ERRORS ❋

LESSON 120

A

1	2	3
expert	comment	**Vocabulary words**
towel	mates	1. count on
wild	teammates	2. mean
wildly	showers	3. block
experts	commenting	4. bury

B

Andrew Plays Harder Ⓐ

Andrew didn't mean to shout at Mean George. But Andrew was frightened. Ⓑ Andrew didn't want to go back to being plain old Andrew Dexter. He wanted to keep on being Handy Andy. Ⓒ Mean George said, "Hey man, you can count on me. Ⓓ I'll give the Titans everything I got. But we want you out there with us. We need you." Ⓔ

"I'll do the best I can," Andrew said.

When Andrew had been as strong as an elephant, he hadn't tried to play as hard as he could have. Ⓕ He didn't want to hurt the other players. So he ran just hard enough to get past the other players. ✿ 2 ERRORS ✿

Now that Andrew's strength was fading, he tried harder. Ⓖ In the next game that Andrew played, he kicked the ball with all his strength. When his first kick was sailing through the air, the announcer said, "That's not much of a kick for Handy Andy, but it's still something to watch. It must have a hang-time of over six seconds. Not bad." Ⓗ

During that game, Andrew was tackled for the first time. He tried to run through the other team instead of kicking the ball. Three players hit him at the same time. Andrew tried to keep his feet under him, but the players brought him down to the ground. Ⓘ

Andrew was tackled three other times during that game. Ⓙ He was tackled four times, but he also scored four touchdowns. When

Andrew got tackled, the other players on the Titans didn't yell at him. They said, "Good try, man. We'll do a better job of blocking for you." Ⓚ

"Thanks," Andrew said.

The game was close, but the Titans won it. The fans cheered for Andrew. They held up signs that said things like HANDY ANDY IS A DANDY, and WITH ANDY THE TITANS ARE NUMBER ONE. But when the game was over, Andrew

Dexter sat on the bench in the locker room. He could hardly catch his breath.Ⓛ His hands were tingling. So were his legs and feet.Ⓜ His body was losing power by the second.Ⓝ

He wiped his sweaty face with a towel. His mind was racing.Ⓞ What would he do now? How long would it be before he lost all his strength? How could the Titans win the championship if he lost his strength? What would the fans do when he went out on the field and couldn't kick the ball any farther than any bank teller could? What would they say when he couldn't run any faster than any other man could run?

The fans would boo. They would throw things onto the field. Andrew could see them in his mind. "Boo," they would yell. "Get that bum off the field." Andrew could almost hear them. He buried his head in the towel.Ⓟ He felt like crying.

"Good game, man."

Andrew didn't look up. He felt the bench bend down as somebody sat next to him. "We're going to do a better job next week," the voice said.Ⓠ It was Mean George. "We didn't do a good job of blocking for you today. Ⓡ But next week, not one of those guys is going to get near you. You'll run down the field like you're all alone."

Andrew wiped his eyes and looked up. "Thanks, George," he said. "But I don't think I'll be able to play next week. I . . ." Ⓢ He shook his head and then buried it in the towel again. Ⓣ Andrew didn't want George to see the tears in his eyes.

"What's this talk about not playing?" George asked, and slapped Andrew on the back. "Of course you're going to play. You're part of this team, right?"

"Yeah," Andrew said, looking up.

"Then you play on this team. I play and you play."

Andrew smiled. "I'll do my best," Andrew said.

"So will we," Mean George said. Ⓤ

•   •   •

There is a difference between players when they play to win and the same players when they are just playing. You could see that

difference during the practices all week long. Ⓥ
The Titans ran their plays with a little more
power, a little more speed, and with all the
players trying harder—a lot harder.

Andrew watched the team and he was
proud of them. They weren't blaming each other
or blaming the coaches. They weren't arguing
and not trying. They were practicing as if they
were champions.

But Andrew didn't feel like a champion. His
strength was no longer that of a quarter horse.
It had faded to the strength of a Mongolian
horse. Ⓦ Of course he was still much stronger
than even the strongest man; however, his
strength was fading. ❊ 13 ERRORS ❊

LESSON 121

A

1	2	3
breakfast	shame	**Vocabulary words**
television	shamed	1. experts
receive	ashamed	2. comment
ache	commenting	3. shower
hinge	wildly	4. still
unusual	teammates	

B

The Titans Play Harder

The Titans practiced hard all week. Andrew kicked the ball four times during the game on Sunday. But not one of his hang-times was six seconds. Ⓐ The shortest hang-time was just under five seconds, and the longest hang-time was just under six seconds. Andrew carried the ball ten times during that game. He scored one touchdown. Ⓑ He tried to make his legs move as fast as they could. And that was very fast. He still had the strength of a small horse. With all that power in his legs, he could run faster than any man alive.Ⓒ He hadn't tried to use all his speed before, but he knew that he could be tackled so he tried to stay away from the players on the other team.Ⓓ ❋ 2 ERRORS ❋

The Titans were one point behind with less than a minute to go.Ⓔ The Titans had the ball. They were fifty meters from the goal line. They decided to try a field goal, with Andrew kicking the ball. The crowd was cheering wildly. If he made this field goal, the Titans would win and they would be in the championship game for the Professional Football League. If he missed, the Titans would lose the game and would not be in the championship game.Ⓕ Andrew's heart was pounding. He kept reminding himself to think about kicking the ball and to think of nothing else. "Watch the ball. Keep your head down. Take two steps. Kick it just under the middle of the ball. Watch the ball. Keep your head down . . ."Ⓖ

The ball was put in place. Andrew took two quick steps forward. He kept his head down. He kicked it, just below the middle of the ball.Ⓗ For a moment he didn't look up. In the distance, he heard the sound of players' shoulder pads hitting other shoulder pads. He heard the whooping sound of the crowd—then a second of almost silence.Ⓘ And then he heard wild cheers.Ⓙ Just as Andrew looked up, the ball sailed between the upright poles.Ⓚ The kick was good. The Titans had scored three more points and had won the game. In two weeks, they would be in the championship game.Ⓛ

The locker room was wild. Reporters and TV cameras were everywhere.Ⓜ There were lights and owners and coaches and players and a lot of shouting: "We're number one!"

"Tell me," a voice said. There were lights in Andrew's eyes. On the other side of the lights was the outline of a TV camera.Ⓝ "Tell me how it feels to be in the championship game."Ⓞ

"I feel great," Andrew said "We have a great team, and we're going to win the championship."

"You'll be playing the Wildcats. Many experts think that they are the strongest team in the league."Ⓟ

Andrew said, "They're a good team, but we beat them once this year already. We're going to try to beat them again."

"That was a great game you played today,"
the announcer said. "A lot of people were
commenting on your speed. We had never seen
you run that fast before. In fact, we didn't know
you had so much speed."

Andrew didn't know what to say. "I had a
lot of help today. My teammates did a great job
of blocking for me."

The yelling and smiling and cheering went
on for nearly an hour. Then the players took

showers, got dressed, and left. The last player in the locker room was Andrew. He sat in front of his locker and said goodbye to each player. Then, when the locker room was empty, Andrew grabbed the handle of his locker and squeezed it as hard as he could.Ⓠ He couldn't make a dent in the steel handle.Ⓡ

"Two weeks," Andrew said to himself, and he felt frightened. "If only I could keep my strength for two weeks."Ⓢ Of course, Andrew wanted to be a star and wanted to have people love him and think he was great. But as he sat there in that still locker room, with only the sound of dripping showers, he wanted the championship for his teammates.Ⓣ He imagined what their faces would look like if they could win the championship. He imagined how they would feel.Ⓤ They would feel proud. And Andrew wanted them to feel proud. But he was beginning to think that he wouldn't be able to help them. His hands and feet were tingling. In only three weeks, his strength had faded from that of an elephant to that of a small horse. What would happen in two more weeks?

❁ 13 ERRORS ❁

LESSON 122

A

1	**2**	**3**
received	signal	**Vocabulary words**
breakfast	grocery	**1.** let somebody down
ached	hinges	**2.** honest
television	unusual	**3.** ashamed
	signaled	**4.** imitate

4

Vocabulary words

1. harm

2. rise

3. completely

4. valuable

B

Andrew Leaves the Team

Andrew's super strength had faded completely.Ⓐ It was now a week before the championship. "Denny," he told the coach. "I can't play in the championship game."Ⓑ

Denny was standing on the sidelines with a whistle in his mouth when Andrew made this announcement. Denny almost swallowed the whistle. Ⓒ Denny coughed and stared at Andrew with big eyes. "You can't <u>what</u>?"

"I can't play," Andrew explained. "I couldn't do the team any good." Ⓓ

"Of course, you can do us good. We need you. I mean, you've been the star of this team ever since you came to us. What's . . ."

✿ 2 ERRORS ✿

Andrew shook his head. "I lost my strength," Andrew said. "I can't kick and I can't run. I won't do you any good."

"Maybe you need to rest for a couple of days," Denny said. "Why don't you take it easy for a few days. We've got time. Your strength will come back. You'll be just as good as you ever were." Ⓔ

"No, coach," Andrew said. "I'm through. I can't play." Andrew shook his head. He tried to say, "I want to thank you for letting me play with the Titans," but his voice wouldn't work. Ⓕ His voice came out like a little squeak. He shook his head, looked down, took a deep breath, and said, "Good luck." Then he ran off the field to the locker room. Ⓖ

Within a couple of minutes, most of the

players were crowding around Andrew. "You can't leave us now," Mean George said. "You are a part of this team. We play, you play."

"I'd like to play," Andrew said, looking down. "But if I'm out there, I won't help you. I'll hurt you. I've got no strength. I'm—"

"Are you hurt?" one of the players asked.

"I can't explain," Andrew said. "But honest, I've got no more strength."

"Hey," George said to the other players. "Let Andy alone. Just get out of here. He'll be all right."

The other players left the locker room. Mean George slapped Andrew Dexter on the back. It hurt. Ⓗ "You just take it easy, Andy," he said. "Everything is going to be all right."

Outside the park four teen-agers were waiting for Andy. He signed their books. One of them said, "The Titans are going to kill the Wildcats next Sunday, right Andy?"

"They're going to play as hard as they can," Andrew said. Ⓘ

But when Sunday came around, Andrew decided not to go to the ball park. He felt ashamed. Ⓙ He didn't want to let the Titans down, but he knew that he couldn't help them. Ⓚ He had planned to watch the game on TV. He felt sick. He hadn't slept well the night before. He imagined the faces of the players and the coaches when he didn't show up. Ⓛ He imagined how they would feel after coming so close to winning the championship. Ⓜ Andrew wanted to see them cheer and shout and hold up their fists as they yelled, "We're number one." But in his mind he could see them walking to the locker room after the game with their heads down. Ⓝ He saw the tears on their faces. He saw the sadness in the faces of the crowd. Ⓞ

Andrew ate breakfast. Ⓟ The phone rang three times but he didn't answer it. The doorbell rang and rang, but he didn't answer the door. Ⓠ He sat there trying to eat his eggs and toast. He wasn't hungry, and eating the toast was like eating paper. He couldn't seem to swallow. Ⓡ At last he gave up and turned on his old television set. Nothing happened. He examined the set, but everything seemed to be all right. Then he thought that the wall plug might not be in right. He wiggled the plug from side to side. The electric cord that went from the plug to the television set was worn out. Ⓢ When Andrew moved the plug from side to side, his finger touched the bare metal inside the electric cord. Ⓣ When his finger touched the bare metal,

Andrew received a terrible electric shock. It knocked him over and almost knocked him out. His teeth ached because he had bitten down so hard from the shock. His arm felt as if somebody had hit it with a hammer. And his fingers tingled. And his feet tingled. And his legs tingled. Ⓤ ❈ 12 ERRORS ❈

LESSON 123

1	2
grocery	**Vocabulary words**
signaled	1. squeals
hinges	2. groan
heavy	3. valuable
heavier	4. completely
coast	5. rise
	6. harm
	7. imitate

B **THE CHAMPIONSHIP GAME**

Andrew had just received a terrible electric shock.Ⓐ His arm and his neck hurt. But he could tell by the tingling feeling in his feet and hands that he had changed.Ⓑ He was strong again. But he couldn't tell how strong. Was he as strong as an elephant again? Or maybe he was as strong as a small horse. Andrew grabbed the doorknob and squeezed it as hard as he could. He did not dent it.Ⓒ Andrew pulled the door without turning the knob. He tore the door off the hinges. **(D)** He was strong all right. He was about as strong as a super strong man.

✳️ 2 ERRORS ✳️

Andrew said to himself, "I might not be as strong as I was, but I'm strong enough to help the Titans." He grabbed his jacket and ran from the place he lived. There were many cars on the street. He thought, "I can probably run to the ball park as fast as I could go in a car." **(E)** So Andrew ran.

Nearly everybody in the city could recognize Andrew. They had seen pictures of him on TV. There were pictures of him in the windows of grocery stores. People wore large buttons with Andrew's picture on them. As Andrew ran down the streets toward the ball park, kids of all ages ran along with him. There were big kids and little kids. At first, about twenty kids ran with him. Then the number continued to grow until hundreds of kids followed Andrew on the way to the ball park. **(F)** Crowds gathered along the streets. They cheered. "Andrew's going to play," they shouted. Earlier that week, TV news stories had told that perhaps Andrew would not play in the championship. **(G)** The reporters had said that Andrew was having some sort of problem and might not play. But when the people saw him running toward the ball park, they knew that he was going to play. "Hooray for Handy Andy," they yelled.

By the time Andrew reached the ball park, he was exhausted.Ⓗ He turned around and waved to the boys and girls who had been running with him. He caught his breath and yelled, "We're going to win." They cheered.

Andrew ran to the locker room. All the members of the team were on the field. The game had started. Andrew could hear the thunder of the crowd.Ⓘ The old man who worked in the locker room said to Andrew, "It looks serious. The Wildcats have already scored a touchdown."Ⓙ

Andrew struggled into his uniform. He ran out of the locker room and into the ball park. As soon as the fans saw him, they let out a great roar. Andrew's muscles were sore from running. He was out of breath. But he was very glad to be on the field. He told himself, "I'm fast and I'm strong. I'll just use my speed and my strength as well as I can."

The coach signaled Andrew to kick a field goal. The announcer's voice came over the loud-speakers. "Now playing for the Titans, Handy Andy Dexter." Ⓚ

The crowd went wild. Fans jumped up and down and beat each other on the back. They squealed and shouted and whistled until they almost lost their voices.

Andrew huddled with the other players. The sound of the crowd was so loud that he could hardly hear what they said. Mean George smiled and said, "When I play, you play, right?"

"Right," Andy said. Ⓛ

Andrew went back as if he was going to kick the ball. Ⓜ The ball came to him and he started to run. He didn't fool anybody on the Wildcat team. They charged him and caught him before he could gain anything. Ⓝ First, two Wildcats hit him. Then a third charged into him, helmet first. That was Smiling Sam. His helmet drove right into Andrew's ribs. Ⓞ Andrew went down and the crowd groaned. Smiling Sam smiled. Ⓟ Then Smiling Sam said,

"Hey, little man, you're not going anywhere today except down." **Q**

Andrew hurt. The Wildcats now had the ball. They moved down the field and scored. They were ahead 14 to 0. **R** The Titans received the ball and moved up the field. But the Wildcats stopped them. Andrew came out to kick the ball. The fans began to clap and stamp their feet.

Andrew went into the huddle. "They think I'm going to kick the ball or run with it," Andrew said. "I think we can fool them if I throw the ball. I don't think the Wildcats will be ready for a pass." Ⓢ

"Let's try a pass," the other Titans said.

Andrew dropped back as if he was going to kick. The ball came to him. The Wildcats charged toward him. Andrew dropped the ball. Ⓣ 🏵 13 ERRORS 🏵

LESSON 124

A

1	2	3
eighty	**Vocabulary words**	**Vocabulary words**
guarded	1. before long	1. groan
decision	2. remains	2. awful
motioned	3. loss	3. frequently
bouncing	4. receive	4. comment
		5. ashamed

B
The End of the Game

The ball was on the ground, bouncing around in front of Andrew.Ⓐ The Wildcats were charging toward him. There was Smiling Sam, with his helmet down and yelling at Andrew, "I got you now."

Andrew made himself think. "Use your speed," he told himself. He picked up the ball and then began to run back. The Wildcats couldn't catch him because he was faster than they were. He ran back farther and farther.

Then he stopped. For a moment, the crowd was silent. Ⓑ Andrew looked down the field, stepped forward, and passed the ball. It was a beautiful pass. ❄ 2 ERRORS ❄

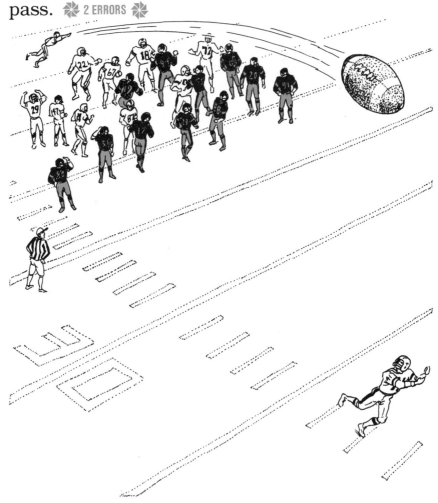

The ball sailed through the air, all the way down the field. The fans were standing. The Wildcats stopped and turned around to watch the ball. All the Titans except one turned around to watch the ball. That Titan ran. He ran toward the goal. And as he ran, he looked over his shoulder. The ball looked as if it was going to go too far.

But the player made a leap, caught the ball, and slid over the goal line. Touchdown. Andrew had just thrown an eighty-meter pass. The Wildcat players were shaking their heads. Andrew was smiling. But Smiling Sam wasn't. "You got lucky," he told Andrew, and made a mean face.©

The Wildcats did not score another touchdown. The Titan players played like champions. They stopped the Wildcats again and again. Late in the game, the Titans scored a field goal. They now had 10 points. The Wildcats had 14 points.⒟

But time was running out.⒠ The Wildcats held the ball and moved slowly down the field. They tried to kick a field goal but a Titan player blocked the kick. The score remained at 14 to 10.⒡ But now there was less than two minutes left in the game. "Let me go in and try to pass again," Andrew said to the coach.

Denny looked at Andrew. "Okay, it's your game. Go and win it." Ⓖ Andrew ran onto the field. He ran into the huddle. "Let's try another pass," Andrew said. Andrew dropped back as if he was going to kick the ball. The ball came to him, and he looked for a Titan player to catch the ball. All the players were being guarded by Wildcats. Ⓗ Andrew had to try to run with the ball. "I got you now," a mean voice said. Ⓘ CRACK—the sound of a helmet driving into Andrew's shoulder pad. He went down for a loss of nearly 10 meters. The crowd groaned. Ⓙ

One of the coaches motioned for the team to try a running play. Ⓚ The Titans lined up quickly. Less than a minute remained in the game. The ball went to one of the players who tried to run wide. Ⓛ The Wildcats were waiting. CRACK. Ⓜ Another loss. The clock continued to move.

Denny motioned from the sideline. He wanted the team to try another pass. Andrew went back. He received the ball. At almost the same time, three Wildcats hit him. Another loss. Ⓝ

The team huddled for the last time. "This is

it," Mean George said.Ⓞ "Let's make it a good one."

Andrew went back. The crowd was not yelling and whooping anymore. In fact, lots of fans were leaving the stands.Ⓟ The fans thought that the Titans had no chance.Ⓠ The ball came to Andrew. He ran back and stopped as if he was going to throw the ball. The Wildcats did not charge after him. They were waiting for the pass. So Andrew made a decision: Run.Ⓡ And he ran.

Andrew put every bit of strength he had into every step. He ran toward the sideline. He outran every player except one.Ⓢ Smiling Sam was charging toward him. "This is it," Andrew told himself. He dropped his shoulder and met Sam's charge. Andrew drove with his feet as hard as he could. CRACK.Ⓣ

The people in the stands were standing. Those fans who had started to leave were coming back. They groaned as the football players hit.Ⓤ The fans saw Smiling Sam fly back. Andrew managed to keep running, but he had been slowed down. Two Wildcat players were near him. He dodged one and ran over the other.Ⓥ There was one more Wildcat that Andrew had to outrun. Andrew gave the run everything he had. And he did it. The crowd went wild. The Titans went wild. With only about 10 seconds left in the game, Andrew had scored the winning touchdown!Ⓦ

• • •

Andrew quit playing for the Titans after the championship game.Ⓧ And he never played football again. He lost his super strength. But the Titans gave him a job working with the coaches.

Andrew didn't mind losing his strength because he had lived the greatest dream that anybody could have lived. And after that year, he didn't daydream as much. Once in a while he would daydream. But he kept his mind on his job because he really liked his job.Ⓨ

One more thing about Andrew: If he goes for a walk, he doesn't walk alone. Before long, a group of kids walk with him. And when they go home, they tell their friends, "Today I was with the greatest football player in the world—Handy Andy."Ⓩ ❀ 15 ERRORS ❀

LESSON 125

1	2	3	4
Eric	halfway	heavier	months
future	somebody	unusual	large
dial	earthquake	coast	caught
wagon	flashlight	sleep	silver
fruit	outfit	asleep	cloth
treasure			

5	6	7
engines	ice	carry
dive	spice	shark
divers	sunk	cabin
lucky	sunken	carrying
diving	spices	sharks

B

Ree Crosses an Ocean

This story has clues in it. See how many questions you can answer.

Liz Jackson lived near a large city that you

have read about. This city is on the west coast of the United States. What's the name of that city?(A)

Liz was a very rich person who raised one kind of animal. This animal has changed over the last 38 million years. It used to be a small animal without hooves. Now it is an animal that everybody knows. What kind of animal did Liz raise?(B)

You learned about five kinds of horses that live today. Name those kinds of horses.(C)

❋ 2 ERRORS ❋

The animals that Liz had were not draft horses. They were not quarter horses, Mongolian horses, or ponies. What kind of horses were they?(D)

Liz wanted to buy a new racehorse. That horse lived in a country that is west of San Francisco. That country is on the other side of the ocean that is next to San Francisco. What ocean is next to San Francisco?(E)

The country with the racehorses was 7 thousand kilometers across the ocean. You have read about that country. What is the name of that country?(F)

Liz wrote to the man who owned the racehorse. The man wrote back that Liz would have to pay 50 thousand dollars for the horse. So Liz paid the owner 50 thousand dollars. She didn't send 50 thousand dollars in money to the man. What did she use to pay the owner of the horse? **G**

Look at the check below and figure out the name of the owner and when Liz wrote the check. **H**

May 21, 1980

Pay to MR. ONO   50 thousand
                                                      dollars

Fifty thousand   ____ dollars

Liz Jackson

The horse's name was Ree. He weighed about as much as most racehorses. So Ree weighed about as much as how many third graders? **I**

Mr. Ono sent Ree to Liz. Ree traveled from

Japan to San Francisco. So in which direction did Ree travel? Ⓙ

Ree did not go in an airplane. And there are no roads across the Pacific Ocean. So how did

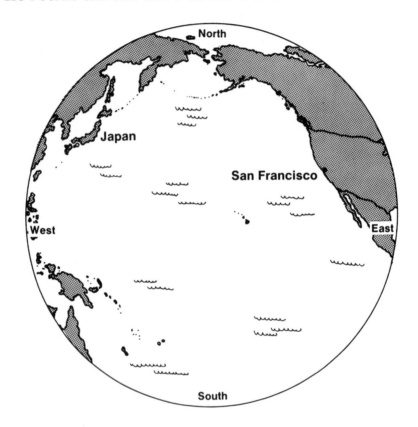

Ree get from Japan to San Francisco? Ⓚ

Ree went on an ocean liner. There were many people on that ship. Some of the people on the ship belonged to a team. That team played on a field that was about 90 meters long.

The players were big and strong. When they played, they wore helmets and shoulder pads. They used a ball that was not round. What kind of team was it?Ⓛ

There was a fly that kept bothering Ree. That fly was the son of the fly that flew farther than any other fly. Name the father.Ⓜ

The ship had a swimming pool on it, and that pool was filled with ocean water. How did that water taste?Ⓝ Is a cup of that water **lighter** or **heavier** than a cup of fresh water?Ⓞ

The passengers on the ship ate a lot. They loved to eat something that comes from palm trees. This thing has two hard shells and sweet milk inside. What is it?Ⓟ

Ree was not the only animal on the ship. There was also a very large animal. It was the strongest land animal in the world. What kind of animal was it?Ⓠ

One of the passengers had an unusual talent. She could tell what things were just by smelling them. Who was that passenger?Ⓡ She was traveling with an investigator. Who was that person?Ⓢ

When the ocean liner came near San

Francisco, something came out to pull the ship to shore. What was that thing? Ⓣ

The tugboat took the ship inside the harbor to a place where ships land. Where do ships land in a harbor? Ⓤ

Liz met the ocean liner. The passengers got off. But Ree and the elephant did not walk off the ship like the other passengers. The crew put a belt around each of these animals. The belt had a large metal plate on it. Then the animals

were picked up by something that sticks to metal things. What picked them up?Ⓥ

Ree didn't like being lifted by the electromagnet. And Ree was glad to be back on the ground.

Liz took Ree to her farm. Ree loves it there. Every day he practices doing the thing that racehorses do best. What does Ree practice?Ⓦ

The stopwatch below shows how long it takes for Ree to run 100 meters. Compare this time with some of Andrew Dexter's best hang-times.Ⓧ ✽ 12 ERRORS ✽

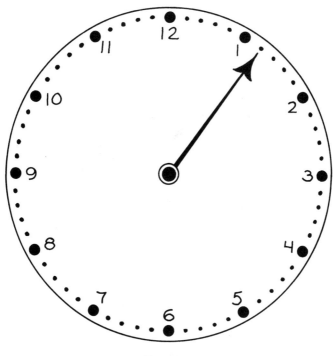

LESSON 126

A

1	2	3	4
carefully	divers	lucky	refrigerators
search	outfit	carrying	earthquake
sometimes	cabin	halfway	imagine
harbor	sharks	asleep	flashlight
trace	diving	somebody	electric

5	6
ruin	**Vocabulary words**
shallow	**1.** sunken ship
difficult	**2.** treasures
special	**3.** rich
equipment	**4.** spices

B

Places You Have Learned About

In today's story, you're going to read about different places in the world. Make sure that you understand the facts you have learned about the world.

Look at the following maps.

Touch A on map 1.Ⓐ What ocean is that?Ⓑ

Touch B on map 1.Ⓒ What country is that?Ⓓ

Name two cities in that country.Ⓔ

What is the name of country C?Ⓕ

What is the name of place D?Ⓖ

What is the name of country E?Ⓗ

Map 1

Touch F on map 2.Ⓘ What is the name of country F?Ⓙ

Map 2

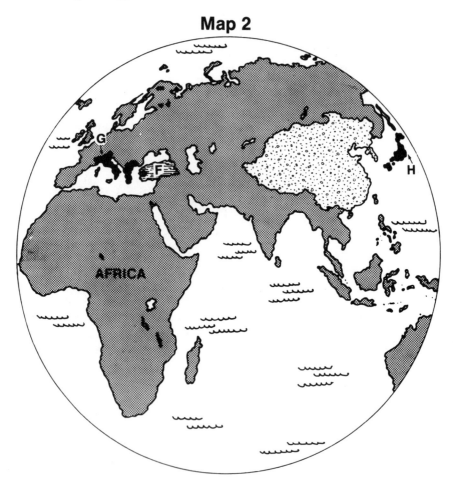

What happened there about 3 thousand years ago?Ⓚ
What's the name of country G?Ⓛ
What's the name of country H?Ⓜ
Name two girls who went to that country.Ⓝ

See if you can find these places on a globe of the world.

- The United States
- Canada
- Mexico
- South America
- Italy
- Turkey
- Japan
- The Pacific Ocean **(O)**

C   Looking for Treasures

Things have changed a lot in the last two hundred years. **(A)** Two hundred years ago, people traveled from place to place by foot, by horse, or by water. **(B)**

Two hundred years ago it took a long, long time to go from one place to another. With a good horse, you could travel 50 kilometers a day. Ⓒ At that speed, it would take you about three months to go from New York to San Francisco. Ⓓ If you fly on a jet plane today, it takes far less time to make the same trip. Ⓔ

Ships went across the ocean two hundred years ago, but the ships were not ocean liners like the ones that Linda and Kathy were on.

❋ 2 ERRORS ❋

The ships of two hundred years ago were sailing ships. They had large sails that caught the wind. Ⓕ The faster ships went 10 kilometers per hour when a good wind was blowing. Ⓖ But the trip from San Francisco to Japan took 30 days. That is a much longer time than the trip would take in an ocean liner. Ⓗ

The ships of two hundred years ago didn't have refrigerators or electric lights. ⓘ Rats and insects would often get into the food and ruin it.

Today, the trip from San Francisco to Japan takes only about 5 days, because the ships of today do not use sails. They have large engines. They can move 65 kilometers per hour. Ⓙ

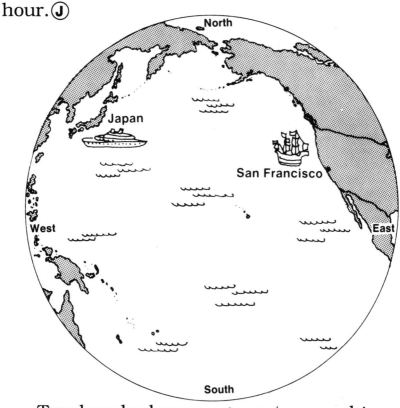

Two hundred years ago, not many ships went between Japan and San Francisco because the trip took so long. But many ships sailed around Italy and Turkey. Ships carried spices, cloth, and things made of gold and silver. 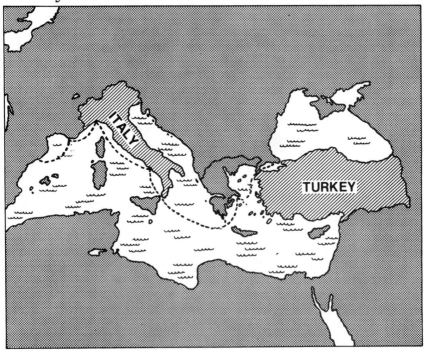Ⓚ Sometimes, ships with great treasures would get caught in a storm. The sails would be torn from the ship. Waves would smash over the ship and it would sink. There are many sunken ships in the oceans around Italy and Turkey.

Divers have found some ships that were carrying great treasures. Can you imagine what it would be like to find such a ship? You dive for days and days in the blue water, looking for signs of a sunken ship but you find nothing. The boat that you dive from moves slowly through the sea, trying to trace the path that the sunken ship took when it was on its way to Italy. Parts of the ocean are deep and parts are shallow. You hope that the ship is found in the shallow parts of the ocean, because it is very difficult to dive in the deep parts. Some parts are so deep that you could not go to the bottom without a very special diving outfit. Ⓛ

Day after day, you dive. Then one day, you see something in the shallow water. It looks like part of an old ship. You swim closer and you see that it is an old ship. You go inside it very carefully. You watch out for sharks and strange fish with long teeth. Ⓜ It's dark inside the sunken ship. You swim to the captain's cabin. Then you see the treasure—boxes with locks on them. Inside are gold coins—piles of them. You are rich. But not many divers who look for sunken ships are as lucky as you are. Ⓝ

Things have changed a lot in the past two hundred years. The trip from New York to Italy would have taken 40 days by sailing ship two hundred years ago. Ⓞ But today, we can go to the airport in New York, get on a jet, and be in Italy 7 hours later. Ⓟ We can call on the phone from New York and tell somebody in Italy that we will be there at 3 o'clock. We can order diving equipment by phone. Ⓠ When we get off the plane in Italy, we can take a cab to the harbor. We can then rent a boat and begin our search for sunken treasure. Ⓡ 🏵 11 ERRORS 🏵

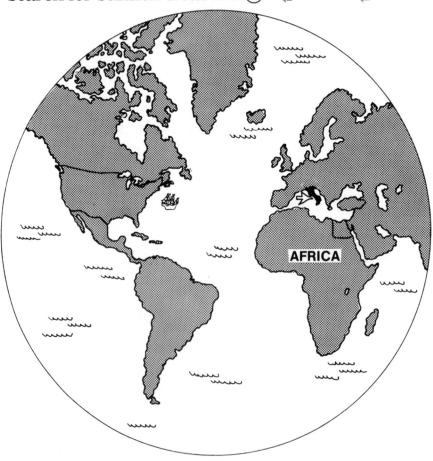

AFRICA

LESSON 127

A

1	2	3
Eric	lights	**Vocabulary words**
somebody	streetlights	1. off in the distance
earthquake	asleep	2. halfway
wagon	Thrig	3. future
clomping	flashlight	4. dial
fruit		

B

ERIC AND TOM FIND A TIME MACHINE Ⓐ

Eric and Tom were with some other boys and girls. They had been at a picnic that was halfway up the mountain. Now they were walking home with the other boys and girls. As they walked down the mountain, they could see the town off in the distance. Ⓑ Eric was tired. "Tom," he said, "let's rest."

Tom said, "I don't think that's a good idea. It's going to get dark pretty soon, and we might get lost." Ⓒ

"That's silly," Eric said. "All we have to do

is follow the path. It goes right back to town. What's the matter? Are you scared?'' ❀ 2 ERRORS ❀

Tom said, "I'm not scared of anything.''

It was very quiet up there on the side of the mountain—very quiet. The lights in the town were coming on. Tom couldn't see the other kids. They were far down the mountain by now. A cool breeze was blowing down the side of the mountain. Ⓓ

Then suddenly there was a loud sound. "Crrrrsssssk.''

Tom jumped up. "Wh—what was that?'' Ⓔ

Again Tom heard the sound: "Crrrrsssssk.'' And then he saw something flash through the sky.

It landed on the side of the mountain right above them. It looked like a great big metal pill. And it was really big. It was as big as some of the trees on the mountain. Ⓕ

"Let's get out of here,'' Tom said. He grabbed Eric's arm, but Eric didn't move. He was standing there with his mouth open. Ⓖ Eric was looking at the pill.

Just then a door on the side of the thing opened, and a man stepped out. He was very

old. He waved to Eric and Tom. "Hello," he
called.

"Let's get out of here," Tom said. Tom's
heart was beating so hard that his shirt was
shaking. Ⓗ

Eric waved to the old man. "Hello," Eric
called. Ⓘ Then Eric started running up the side
of the mountain toward the metal pill.

"Come back," Tom called. But Eric ran up
to the old man. The old man was sitting on the

ground. He did not look well. Ⓙ He was wearing a strange metal coat.

"Who are you?" Eric asked.

The old man said, "My name is Thrig." Ⓚ

Eric said, "Where do you live?"

Thrig said, "I live on Earth. But I live in a different time than you." Ⓛ

Tom and Eric looked at each other. Tom thought, "How can somebody live in a different time?"

Thrig then told Eric and Tom a very strange story. Thrig told them that he lived in the year 2380. Ⓜ

A • **The year Thrig was from**

B • **Now**

C • **The year the United States became a country**

Tom said, "The year 2380 will not be here for 4 hundred years. That year is 4 hundred years in the future." (N)

Thrig nodded. "Yes, I live in the future," he said. He told the boys that he had made a time machine. This machine could take him into the past. He had just gone from the year 2380 to the year it is now. (O) Thrig had gone back in time 4 hundred years. The large thing that looked like a pill was his time machine. (P)

Thrig stood up and shook his head. "But now I cannot go back to the year 2380," he said. "I am old. And when the machine goes through time, it puts a great force on your body. I do not think that I have enough strength to return to 2380." (Q) Thrig said, "I will spend the rest of my life here. I will never see my friends again."

Thrig looked very sad. "And now I must rest. The trip through time has made me very tired." Thrig sat down again and closed his eyes.

"He's asleep," Eric said after a moment. "He's sound asleep." Then Eric walked toward the time machine. (R)

Tom grabbed Eric's arm and said, "Let's get out of here before something happens."

Eric laughed. He said, "That time machine won't bite you." Eric pulled away and started toward the door.Ⓢ

Tom ran after Eric. He caught up just as Eric was going through the door of the giant machine.

The inside of the time machine was filled with dials and lights. There were red lights and green lights and orange lights. There were big dials and little dials. There were dials that buzzed and dials that clicked. "Let's get out of here," Tom said.Ⓣ

Eric walked over to a seat in the middle of the machine. He sat down. As soon as he sat down, the door closed. ''Swwwwwshshshs.'' **Ⓤ**

Eric grabbed one of the handles. ''I wonder what this handle does.''

''Don't touch it,'' Tom said. ''Don't touch it.'' **Ⓥ**

Eric pulled the handle down a little bit. Suddenly more lights started going on. Dials started moving and clicking and buzzing. And then Tom felt a great force. He could feel it push against his face and his chest. **Ⓦ**

''We—we're going through time,'' Tom announced.

He heard Eric's voice. It sounded very far away. ''Oh no,'' Eric cried. ''I don't want to go back in time. No . . .''

And then everything was quiet. Tom's ears hurt. The dials slowed down. Most of the lights stopped flashing. **Ⓧ**

Eric stood up and the door opened. **Ⓨ** The boys looked outside. For a long time they looked. They could not believe what they saw. **Ⓩ**

 15 ERRORS

LESSON 128

1	2	3
Egypt	fruit	**Vocabulary words**
pyramid	wagon	1. clomping
recorder	streetlights	2. downtown
palace	shelf	3. earthquake
		4. leans

B   More about Time

In today's story, you'll find out what year Tom and Eric went to in the time machine.

That year was not in the future.Ⓐ

So you know that they did not go to some of the years below. Tell which years they did not go to.Ⓑ

a. 2450   b. 2000   c. 1880   d. 1900
e. 2600   f. 2380   g. 1490   h. 1776

Tom and Eric didn't go into the future. So you know that they went into the _____.Ⓒ

A ● **The year Thrig was from**

B ● **The year Eric and Tom started their trip**

They didn't go very far back into the past.
They didn't go back two hundred years. What
year would they have gone to if they went back
two hundred years? **(D)**

Touch dot B on the time line. **(E)** That is the
year that Eric and Tom started their trip. What
year is that? **(F)**

Touch dot A. **(G)** That is the year that Thrig
was from. What year is that? **(H)**

Is that year in the past or the future? **(I)**

About how many years in the future? **(J)**

C

The San Francisco Earthquake Ⓐ

Tom and Eric looked out of the time machine. They were on the side of a mountain, but it was not the same mountain they were on before Eric had pulled the handle in the time machine.

Tom could see a large city down below them. Lights were on all over the city, but they did not look very bright. Ⓑ

"Let's go down there," Eric said.

Tom said, "Remember, we don't know where we are. Let's be careful."

It was a long way down the mountain. By the time the boys got to the city, the sky was very dark. The city had buildings and streets, but there was something strange about the city.

❋ 2 ERRORS ❋

"I know what's funny," Tom said. "Most of the streets are made of dirt." Tom pointed to the streetlights. "Those are gas streetlights," he said. "Those are the kind of streetlights they had a long time ago." Ⓒ

Just then a clomping sound came down the street. Ⓓ The boys hid behind a fence. The sound came from a wagon that was pulled by a horse. Ⓔ

After the wagon went by, Tom said, "We've gone back in time, all right."

Eric said, "Things don't look very different."

Tom said, "You don't hear any cars or trucks, do you?" Ⓕ

Then Tom said, "We'd better find a place to sleep."

They found a barn outside the city. They slept in the hay. Tom did not sleep very well. He had bad dreams, and he kept waking up. Ⓖ

Very early in the morning, they started to walk toward the center of the city. On the way they saw a newspaper in the street. They looked at the first page of the newspaper. Ⓗ Here are the words that were at the top of the page: "San Francisco Times." Ⓘ

Eric asked, "What's San Francisco?" Ⓙ

"San Francisco is a city," Tom said. "It is near the Pacific Ocean." Tom looked at the date at the top of the newspaper: April 18, 1906. Ⓚ Tom felt dizzy. "We've gone back in time almost a hundred years," Tom said to himself. "1906.

Something happened in San Francisco in 1906, but I can't remember what." Ⓛ

Tom looked up. Three boys were standing on the sidewalk. They were wearing funny pants that stopped just below their knees. They were laughing at Tom and Eric. The tallest boy said to Tom, "You sure look funny wearing those funny clothes."

Tom looked at his clothes. They didn't look funny to him. Ⓜ

"Let's get out of here," Eric said. "Let's go downtown."

The boys walked past blocks and blocks of buildings. Some of the buildings were little and some were pretty big. But most of them were made of wood.

People were riding horses or they were riding in wagons pulled by horses. Some boys and girls rode bicycles. Tom and Eric saw only one car. It was one of the very first cars ever made. When the car went by, a horse went wild and started to run down the street. Ⓞ The horse was pulling a wagon full of fruit. Fruit spilled all over the street. Tom and Eric picked up some apples. Ⓟ

Just then, the street shook. The ground moved to one side. It moved so fast that Eric fell down. Then the ground moved the other way, and Tom could see a large crack starting to form right in the middle of the street.Ⓠ

Tom yelled, "I remember what happened in 1906. The earthquake! The San Francisco earthquake!"Ⓡ

Tom could hardly hear his own voice. People were screaming and running from buildings. A building on the corner started to lean and then it fell into the street. The crack in the middle of the street suddenly got wider and longer. The crack ran down the street. A horse and wagon slid and fell into the crack.

Suddenly, fires started to break out all along the crack. The crack had broken the gas lines, and now the gas was burning. Buildings were burning. The ground was shaking. People were running and screaming. Buildings were falling. "We've got to get out of here," Tom yelled.Ⓢ

Hundreds of men and women were running down the street. They pushed this way and that way. The ground shook again. Another great crack formed in the street. It ran across the street and ran right between Eric and Tom. The crack got wider and wider. And suddenly Eric fell into the crack.Ⓣ   ❋ 12 ERRORS ❋

LESSON 129

A

1	**2**	**3**
palace	fallen	**Vocabulary words**
pyramids	earth	**1.** tape recorder
Egypt	finally	**2.** flashlight
shelf	chain	**3.** blade
throne	mountain	

B

More about Time

In today's story, you will find out more about the trip that Eric and Tom took through time.

A • **The year Thrig was from**

B • **The year Eric and Tom started their trip**
C • **The year Eric and Tom were in San Francisco**

Touch dot B.Ⓐ That is the year Eric and Tom started their trip. What year did they start?Ⓑ

Touch dot A.Ⓒ That's the year Thrig was from. What year was that?Ⓓ

Touch dot C.Ⓔ That was the year Eric and Tom were in San Francisco. What year was that?Ⓕ

You learned about something that was first made around the year 1900.Ⓖ

C

Egypt

The story that you will read today tells about Egypt. Ⓐ Egypt is a country that is close to Italy. Ⓑ

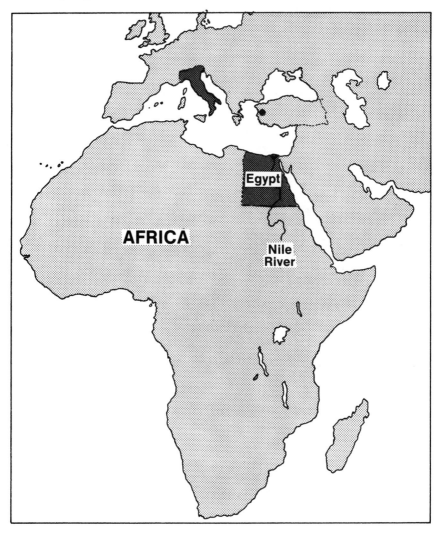

Here are some facts about Egypt.

- Egypt is a country with oil wells.
- Some buildings in Egypt are over five thousand years old.
- Some buildings in Egypt are called **pyramids.** Here's a picture that shows some pyramids. Ⓒ

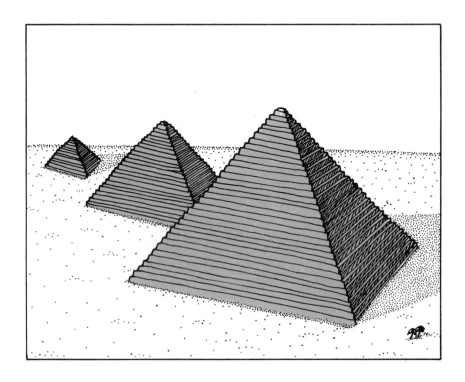

- Egypt has a great river running through it. That river is named the Nile. Touch the Nile River on the map. Ⓓ

D

Eric and Tom in Egypt Ⓐ

Eric had fallen into the crack in the ground. But Tom held on to Eric's hand. Tom looked down into the crack. It seemed to go down forever. Ⓑ Tom almost slipped. He pulled and pulled, and he finally pulled Eric out of the crack.

Then they ran. They pushed through crowds. From time to time, the earth would shake and knock them down. They ran past houses that were burning. Ⓒ They ran past houses that had fallen over. Ⓓ

When they got to the mountain outside the city, they looked back. The whole city was burning. They could hear people screaming in the distance. They were both tired. But they kept running up the side of the mountain to the time machine. ✿ 2 ERRORS ✿

"Now," Tom said, "let's figure out a way to get back to the right time." Ⓔ

They went inside the time machine. Dials were clicking and lights were flashing inside the machine. Tom sat down in the seat. Ⓕ The door shut: "Swwwshshsh." Tom pointed to the handle that Eric had pulled. "This makes the time machine work," Tom said.

Eric said, "When I pulled down on it, we went back in time."

Tom said, "I'll bet we will go forward in time if we push the handle up." **G**

"Push it up," Eric said.

Tom grabbed the handle. It felt very cold. He tried to push it up, but it wouldn't move. "It's stuck," he said. "The handle won't move."

Eric pushed on the handle, but the outcome was the same. **H**

"It's got to move," Tom said. He pushed and pulled with all his strength. Suddenly, the handle moved down. A force pushed against him. **I**

Eric's voice sounded far away as he said, "Oh no."

Lights went on and off. Dials clicked and buzzed. Then things began to quiet down. **J** Eric said, "I'm afraid to look outside."

Tom stood up. The door opened. **K** It was very bright outside. At first, Tom couldn't believe what he saw.

The time machine was on a side of a

mountain above a great river. There were many rafts and boats on the river. But they did not look like any rafts and boats that Tom had ever seen before. Next to the river was a city. But it did not look like any city that Tom had ever seen before. All the buildings in the city were white. And next to the city were two great pyramids. One of them was already built and the other one was almost finished. Hundreds of men were dragging great stones toward this pyramid.Ⓛ

"We're in Egypt," Tom said. "We're in Egypt five thousand years ago! Look over there. The men are building a pyramid."Ⓜ

"What are pyramids for?" Eric asked.

Tom said, "When a king dies, they put him in a pyramid along with all of his slaves and his goats and everything else he owned."Ⓝ

Eric said, "Let's take a nap. When it's dark, we'll go down to the city."Ⓞ

So Tom and Eric slept. They woke up just as the sun was setting. Tom looked inside the time machine for a flashlight. He found one on a shelf. Next to it was a tiny tape recorder. He put the flashlight in one pocket and the tape recorder in the other.

Then Eric and Tom started down the mountain. They were very hungry. Down, down they went. They found a road at the bottom of the mountain. The road led into the city.

It was very quiet and very dark in the city. Ⓟ Tom took out his flashlight and was ready to turn it on.

*Suddenly, a soldier was standing in front of Tom. He had metal bands on his arms and he held a large sword. He pointed the sword at Tom. "Ha hu ru," he said. Ⓠ

Tom looked at the soldier and said, "I don't know what you said." Ⓡ

The soldier moved the sword closer to Tom. Tom could see little marks on the blade. He could see a big scar on the soldier's hand. "Ha hu ru," the soldier said again. Ⓢ

Eric said, "He looks mad. We'd better do something."

The soldier yelled, "Ha hu ru," and shook his sword. But Tom* still couldn't understand him.

The blade of the sword was only inches from Tom's face. Tom did not know what to do. Ⓣ ❀ 12 ERRORS ❀

LESSON 130

1	2	3
Nile River	remember	**Vocabulary words**
chain	knees	1. lead somebody
sword	power	2. bow
soldier	guards	3. palace
toward	building	4. smash
		5. throne

B

More about Time

Look at the time line.

Touch dot B. Ⓐ Dot B shows the year that Eric and Tom found the time machine. What year was that? Ⓑ

Touch dot A. Ⓒ Dot A shows the year that Thrig was from. What year was that? Ⓓ

Touch dot C. Ⓔ Dot C shows the year that Eric and Tom were in San Francisco. When was that? Ⓕ

Touch dot D. Ⓖ Dot D shows the year that

A ● The year Thrig was from

B ● The year Eric and Tom started their trip
C ● The year Eric and Tom were in San Francisco
D ● The year the United States became a country

E ● When the story of Troy took place

F ● When Eric and Tom were in Egypt

the United States became a country. What year was that?Ⓗ

Touch dot E.Ⓘ Dot E shows when the story of Troy took place. How long ago did that take place?Ⓙ

Touch dot F.Ⓚ Dot F shows when Eric and Tom were in Egypt. How long ago was that?Ⓛ

C Eric and Tom Meet the King of Egypt Ⓐ

The soldier was shaking a sword at Tom. "Ha hu <u>ru</u>," the soldier yelled, and Tom saw the sword move toward him. Tom put his hand over his face. He didn't remember that he had a flashlight in his hand. Without thinking, Tom turned the flashlight on.

When the soldier saw the light, he stepped back. He put his sword on the ground. "On ton urub," he said very softly. Ⓑ The soldier got down on his hands and knees. "On ton urub," he said again.

Eric said, "He thinks that you have some kind of great power. <u>Maybe</u> he thinks you are a <u>sun god</u>." Ⓒ ❊ 2 ERRORS ❊

Tom smiled. "Maybe it will be fun to be a sun god."

Eric said, "Be careful, Tom." Ⓓ

Tom walked over to the soldier. "Take me to your <u>king</u>," he said. "The sun god wants to meet the king of Egypt." Ⓔ Tom pointed toward the middle of the city.

The soldier stood up. He bowed three times. Then he started to lead the boys down the streets. Soon they came to a large palace. There were hundreds of steps in front of the palace.

The soldier went up to three guards in front of the palace. The soldier talked and pointed to Tom. Then one guard walked up to the boys. The guard backed away and bowed three times. Ⓕ

Eric said, "I think he wants us to follow him."

So Tom and Eric followed the guard. Up the steps they went. Up, up, up to the great doors that led inside the palace.

"What a palace," Tom said. He had never been in a building so big. The hall seemed blocks and blocks long. And a soldier was standing every two meters on each side of the hall. There were hundreds of soldiers in that hall. Ⓖ

The guard walked down the hall. Tom and Eric followed. At last they walked through another huge door. They were now inside a great room looking at an old man. He was sitting on the floor with a large chain around his neck. At the end of the chain was a large metal ball. The ball looked like the sun. Ⓗ

The soldier said something to the old man. The old man looked at the boys for a long time. Then he smiled and stood up. He walked over and held out his hand. "Ura bustu," he said.

"He wants the flashlight," Eric said. "Don't give it to him."

"Don't worry," Tom said. Tom shook his head no. Then he pointed the flashlight at the old man's neck chain. Tom turned on the flashlight. The sun became bright.Ⓘ

The old man held his hand over the sun. "On ton urub," he said. "On ton urub."Ⓙ

Eric said, "Now he thinks that you're a sun god."

Tom walked over to the guard and snapped his fingers. "Eat, eat," Tom said, and pretended to eat.Ⓚ

"Hem stroo," the soldier said smiling. "Hem stroo." The soldier ran from the room and down the hall.Ⓛ

Suddenly, many people came into the room. They were carrying all kinds of food. Tom looked at all of the food in front of him. He saw a large bowl. It had milk in it. Tom said, "I'll bet it's goat milk."

Eric tasted it. He made a face. "It's warm," he said. "Why don't they have <u>cold</u> milk?" **M**

Tom said, "Their milk isn't cold because they don't have any way to keep it cold. Nobody had refrigerators until after the year 1900." **N**

Tom and Eric ate and ate. Then the old man took Tom and Eric to their room. Tom put his flashlight in his pocket and went to sleep.

In the morning the old man took the boys to a great room at the end of the hall. Inside the room a young man sat on a throne. The throne was made of gold and silver. **O**

Eric said, "That young man must be the king."

"Hara uha <u>ho</u>," the king said. His voice was sharp.Ⓟ

Tom and Eric walked to the throne. The king stood up and walked to a window in the room. He pointed to the sunlight that was coming through the window. "Tasa u horu," he said. Then he pointed to Tom. "Umul hock a huck."Ⓠ

Tom knew what the king wanted. Tom pointed the flashlight at the king and pressed the button on the flashlight. But nothing happened. The flashlight did not go on. Tom pressed the button again. The outcome was the same.Ⓡ

"Aso uhuck," the king said. He snapped his fingers and two soldiers came forward. One of them grabbed Tom and the other grabbed Eric.Ⓢ

The king grabbed the flashlight from Tom's hand and threw it to the floor. It smashed. Tom looked at the flashlight. Then he looked up into the face of the king. The king looked very, very mean. ❉ 13 ERRORS ❉

LESSON 131

1	**2**	**3**
language	Nile River	continued
saber-toothed	Spain	spices
Columbus	recorded	pyramid
mammoth	raft	broken

4

Vocabulary words

1. fur
2. grain

B   Eric and Tom Leave Egypt

A soldier was holding Tom. The flashlight was on the floor. It was broken. Tom could not play sun god anymore. Ⓐ

The king was yelling at the man with the chain and sun around his neck. Suddenly, Tom got an idea. He reached into his pocket and took out the tape recorder. He pressed the button. The king was saying, "Ra hu hub haki." Ⓑ

Tom held the tape recorder up high and played back what he had recorded. "Ra hu hub haki." The king stopped yelling. He looked at Tom. The soldier let go of Tom. Tom ran the tape back and played it again. He played it as loud as it would go. "Ra hu hub haki."

✿ 2 ERRORS ✿

The king smiled and bowed. Ⓒ Tom walked up to the king. He pressed the button so that the tape recorder would record again. Then he said, "I am the sun god, and I have your words on this tape."

The king bowed and said, "Un uh, run du."

Tom played the tape back as loud as he could. Ⓓ

Eric said, "Tom, let's get out of here before the tape recorder breaks. Remember what happened to the flashlight."

Eric and Tom walked down the long, long hall. They did not look back. They walked through the great doors of the palace. Then they started to run.Ⓔ They ran down the stairs—down, down. When they came to the bottom of the stairs, they kept on running. They ran down the streets of the city until they came to the river. Then they stopped. They were both tired. People around them were pointing at them and talking.Ⓕ

Tom said, "That's the Nile River." He pointed to one of the huge rafts on the river. "That raft is carrying hundreds and hundreds of sacks of grain."Ⓖ Tom continued, "One raft can carry as much grain as a hundred wagons could carry."Ⓗ

"Why don't they use trucks?" Eric asked.Ⓘ

Tom laughed. "Nobody had trucks until around 1900."

Eric looked at the rafts on the river. They carried all kinds of things—animals, furs, spices, food, and even great big stones the size of a car. "What are they going to do with those stones?" he asked.

Tom said, "They will use them to build a pyramid. They need thousands of stones to build one pyramid." Ⓙ

Just then a soldier came up to Eric and Tom. He held out his sword. "Ra uh hack stuck," he said. Ⓚ

Tom held up the tape recorder and played back the soldier's words. "Ra uh hack stuck." The soldier backed away. Ⓛ

Tom and Eric found a path that led up the mountain. They walked up and up. The mountain was very steep, and by the time they got to the time machine, they were tired and hungry.

They went inside the time machine. Tom sat down in the seat. Ⓜ "This time," he said, "I'm going to make the handle go up so we can go forward in time." Ⓝ

"I hope so," Eric said. "I don't want to go back any further in time."

Tom pushed up on the handle. It did not move. He moved in the seat. Then, suddenly, the handle moved up. Dials started to click and buzz. Lights went on and off. Tom felt the force against his face.

Then everything was quiet except for a few dials that were clicking and buzzing. Tom heard something scratching on the outside of the time machine. He stood up. The door opened. And something started to walk inside the time machine. It was a great big yellow lion.

❄ 10 ERRORS ❄

LESSON 132

1	2	3
Columbus	mammoth	**Vocabulary words**
saber-toothed	hill	tame
language	downhill	
doorway	muscles	
	teacher	

B Greece and Spain

In today's story, you will read about Greece. The map below shows Greece as it is today.

Greece is a small country that is near Italy. It is north of Egypt. It is west of Turkey. Ⓐ

You already know about something that happened in Greece a long time ago. Ⓑ

In a few lessons, you will read about another country that is near Italy and Greece. The name of that country is Spain. Touch Spain on the map. Ⓒ

C

Eric and Tom in Greece

A lion was in the doorway of the time machine. The lion was walking toward Tom. Tom could see the muscles in the lion's legs as it walked. Ⓐ

Suddenly, a man came through the doorway of the time machine. He was wearing a long white robe. He stared at the lights and dials. The man put his hand on the lion's back. The lion looked up at the man. Ⓑ

"That lion is tame," Eric said. Ⓒ

The man said something to Tom and Eric, but they could not understand the man's language. The man pointed toward the door of the time machine. Tom and Eric followed him outside. ❀ 2 ERRORS ❀

The time machine was in a place that looked like a park. There were trees and grass. A few young men were standing outside. Tom said, ''I think we are in a school of long, long ago. I think we are in Greece thousands of years ago.''

Eric said, ''We sure are a long way from home.''

The man in the robe said something and then pointed to a large table covered with food. **(D)** ''He wants us to eat,'' Tom said.

''Good deal,'' Eric said. ''I'm really hungry. I don't even care if they give us warm milk.'' **(E)**

After Tom and Eric ate, they watched the young men and their teacher. The teacher sat on a stone bench. The young men sat on the ground around him. The teacher asked questions. The young men would try to answer the questions. The teacher asked more questions. **(F)**

Tom said, ''I think they're learning how to argue. **(G)** They learn to argue so they can learn

to think clearly. The teacher wants to show them that they don't know as much as they think they know." Ⓗ

"Why is he doing that?" Eric asked.

Tom replied, "So they will think about things."

Just then a man on a horse rode up. He stopped on the top of a hill near the school.

Then he called to the teacher. The teacher walked up the hill. Tom and Eric followed. Tom could see the ocean from the top of the hill. The man on the horse pointed to hundreds of ships on the ocean.

Tom and Eric looked at the ships. Eric said, "I have never seen so many ships in one place before. Where do you think they're going?" Ⓘ

Tom said, "I think we're in Greece three thousand years ago. There were many cities in Greece at that time. Some of those cities went to war because a queen of one city ran away with somebody from Troy." Ⓙ Tom continued. "So part of Greece went to war and sent a thousand ships into battle." Tom pointed to the ships below. "I think those are the ships that are going to Troy."

Some ships were loaded with soldiers and horses. Others carried large machines for throwing rocks through the air. Tom said, "Thousands of men will die in the battle with Troy. And that battle will go on for many years." Ⓚ

In the distance, Tom and Eric could hear the sounds of soldiers singing. Tom and Eric watched for a few minutes. The teacher standing next to them shook his head. He looked very sad. Ⓛ

"I think we'd better get out of here," Tom said. "I want to get back home."

Tom and Eric started to walk back to the time machine. The teacher and the young men were still on the hill.

Tom and Eric went inside the time machine. Tom sat down in the seat. The door closed. Then Tom said, "I wish I knew how to make this time machine work right."

Eric said, "Let me try. You didn't do very well the last time you tried."

Eric reached for the handle. Tom tried to push Eric's hand away, but Eric had a good grip on the handle. Suddenly, the handle moved down—all the way down. Ⓜ Before Tom could pull the handle back up, he felt the force against his face and ears.

"Oh no!" Eric yelled. Then everything seemed to go dark. Ⓝ　✾ 11 ERRORS ✾

LESSON 133

1	2	3
saber-toothed	breathing	**Vocabulary words**
downhill	terrible	1. mound
again	giant	2. spikes
against	modern	3. snort
		4. mammoth
		5. crunching

B

More about Time

Look at the time line. Touch dot B. Ⓐ That dot shows when Eric and Tom started their trip. What year was that? Ⓑ

Touch dot A. Ⓒ That dot shows the year that Thrig was from. What year was that? Ⓓ

Touch dot C. Ⓔ That dot shows when Eric and Tom were in San Francisco. What year was that? Ⓕ

Touch dot D. Ⓖ That dot shows when Eric

and Tom were in Greece. How long ago was that?Ⓗ

    Touch dot E.Ⓘ That dot shows when Eric and Tom were in Egypt. How long ago was that?Ⓙ

A • **The year Thrig was from**

B • **The year Eric and Tom were from**
C • **Eric and Tom in San Francisco**

D • **Eric and Tom in Greece**

E • **Eric and Tom in Egypt**

C

Forty Thousand Years Ago Ⓐ

The force was so great that Tom's ears began ringing. He had trouble breathing. He couldn't talk. Ⓑ Then things inside the time machine looked brighter again. The dials and lights blinked and flashed.

"I hate to look outside," Eric said. His voice sounded funny.

Tom rubbed his eyes. "That handle went down all the way," Tom said.

Eric stood up and the door opened. The air was cool, and some trees looked a little different from any Tom had ever seen.

Eric and Tom stood outside the time machine for a few minutes. They looked in all directions, but they couldn't see any people. At first they didn't see any animals either. But then they heard a terrible roar. ❉ 2 ERRORS ❉

A moment later, three very small horses charged down a hill. Ⓒ They were no bigger than ponies, but they looked different.

The horses ran through the long grass. Another animal was running behind them. It was very fast, but not as tall as the horses. Tom could see it leaping through the tall grass, but he couldn't get a good look at it. Suddenly, the horses turned and ran downhill. The animal that had been chasing them stopped and stood on top of a mound. Ⓓ Now Tom and Eric could see the animal clearly.

Eric said, "Do you see what I see?"

Tom didn't take his eyes from the animal. "Yes," he said.

The animal had a short tail, and two long teeth that stuck down like spikes. Tom said, "I think we've gone back about forty thousand years from our time. Ⓔ I think we're looking at a saber-toothed tiger." Ⓕ

Tom said, "Those other animals were the kind of horses that lived forty thousand years ago."

Just as Eric started to say something, a loud snorting noise came from the other side of the time machine. Ⓖ The boys turned around. The animal making the noise was a giant mammoth—an elephant with long fur and great tusks. Ⓗ It held its trunk high in the air. Its eyes were bright and it didn't look friendly. Ⓘ "Let's get out of here," Tom said. The boys ducked

inside the time machine. Tom ran to the seat and sat down, but just as the door was closing, the mammoth charged into it. It made a terrible crunching sound. And the door wouldn't close. Ⓙ The door was open about half a meter. Ⓚ The mammoth stuck its trunk through the open door and let out a great trumpeting sound. Ⓛ

The mammoth suddenly backed up and began to run. Some humans were running down the hill. Ⓜ The humans were dressed in animal skins. They were shouting and running.

The mammoth ran downhill. "Let's get out of here," Tom said.

The humans were coming closer to the time machine. They were about fifty meters away. They were shouting and growling. Ⓝ Tom had picked up a long branch. He was trying to bend the door so that it would close.

"Hurry," Eric said.

Two men were running toward the door. "Push on the door," Tom yelled. He was trying to bend the bottom of the door with the branch.

The men were only a few meters from the door now. Tom could smell them. "Push," Tom said. "Push."

"Blump." One of the men had thrown a rock and hit the side of the time machine. "Blump, blump, blump." More rocks.

One of the men grabbed the door. Tom could see his face and his teeth. Ⓞ ❋ 10 ERRORS ❋

LESSON 134

1	2
against	**Vocabulary words**
America	**1.** modern
straighten	**2.** English
huge	**3.** old-time
straightened	**4.** grin

B

More about Time

Look at the time line. Touch dot B. Ⓐ That dot shows when Eric and Tom started their trip. What year was that? Ⓑ

Touch dot A. Ⓒ That dot shows the year that Thrig was from. What year was that? Ⓓ

Touch dot C. Ⓔ That dot shows when Eric and Tom were in San Francisco. What year was that? Ⓕ

Touch dot D. Ⓖ That dot shows when Eric and Tom were in Greece. How long ago was that? Ⓗ

Touch dot E. Ⓘ That dot shows when Eric

and Tom were in Egypt. How long ago was that? Ⓙ

Touch dot F. Ⓚ That dot shows when Eric and Tom saw the cave people. How long ago was that? Ⓛ

A● **The year Thrig was from**

B● **The year Eric and Tom were from**

C● **Eric and Tom in San Francisco**

D● **Eric and Tom in Greece**

E● **Eric and Tom in Egypt**

F● **Eric and Tom see cave people**

C   Eric and Tom in the City of the Future(A)

"Push," Tom yelled.(B) Just then a large rock hit the door. And suddenly the door closed. The rock must have straightened the door so that it could close again.(C)

*The door started to open again. "Quick," Tom said. "Sit in the chair so the door closes."

Eric ran to the seat and sat down. The door stayed closed now.

"Blump, blump." Rocks were hitting the side of the time machine.

"Push the handle up," Tom said. Eric bounced around in the seat and pushed on the handle. Rocks continued to hit the time machine. ❈ 2 ERRORS ❈

Suddenly, the handle went up—far up. Tom almost fell down from the force. Then he almost passed out.(D) After a few moments, the force died down. Eric stood up, and the door opened.

The* time machine was next to a huge building—the tallest building that Tom had ever seen. There were buildings all around. Tom could not see the sun, only buildings. There were no streets and no cars—just buildings.

People were walking near the time machine.
They wore funny clothes that seemed to shine.

Eric said, "We must have gone into the
future." **E**

A young man walked by the time machine.
Tom said, "Can you help us?" The man looked
at Tom and said, "Selip." Then he walked
away. **F**

Tom and Eric stopped person after person.

But every person said, "Selip," and walked away. Finally, Tom stopped an old man. "Can you help us?" Tom asked.

The old man smiled. Very slowly he said, "I . . . will . . . try." **G**

Tom and Eric grinned. **H** Tom said, "Can you help us work our time machine?"

The old man made a face. Then he said, "Talk . . . slower."

Tom said, "Can . . . you . . . help . . . us . . . work . . . this . . . machine?" **I**

The old man said, "No. We . . . have . . . machines . . . that . . . fix . . . machines. People . . . do . . . not . . . fix machines." **J**

Tom said, "Can . . . you . . . get . . . a machine . . . to help . . . us . . . work . . . our . . . time machine?"

The old man said, "That . . . time machine . . . is too old. We do not have . . . machines . . . that work . . . on such . . . old . . . time machines." **K**

Tom felt sad. He and Eric would have to figure out how to work the machine by themselves. **L**

The old man made a face. He thought for a

few moments. Then he said, "What . . . year . . . are you . . . from?" Eric told him. Ⓜ

The old man thought and thought. "We . . . are . . . four thousand years . . . after your . . . time." Ⓝ

"Thank you," Tom said to the old man. "Thank you . . . very . . . much."

The old man smiled.

Eric said, "Why . . . do you speak . . . English? Nobody else . . . speaks . . . English."

The old man said, "I study . . . old, old languages. You . . . are very . . . lucky . . . to find me. No . . . other . . . people in the city . . . know . . . your language." Ⓞ

Eric asked, "What does . . . selip . . . mean?"

The old man said, "Selip . . . means this: I am . . . very sorry . . . that I cannot . . . help you. I . . . do not understand . . . your words. Good day."

Tom said, "Do you mean . . . that . . . one little . . . word . . . like selip . . . means all that?"

"Yes," the old man said. "People . . . who live . . . in this time . . . do not have . . . to think . . . very much. So . . . the language . . . that they use . . . is very . . . simple. They . . . let the machines . . . do all . . . of their . . . thinking . . . for them.'' Ⓟ

Eric and Tom got into the time machine. Tom sat down and the door closed. Tom pulled the handle about halfway down. The dials buzzed. Lights went on and off. The force pushed against Tom's ears. Then it died down. Ⓠ

Tom stood up. The door opened. And outside the door, Tom could see water. On that water was a ship. But it wasn't a modern ship. It was an old-time sailing ship.　❀ 10 ERRORS ❀

LESSON 135

1

Columbus

America

Viking

angry

replied

2

Vocabulary words

1. shack

2. flat

3. lie

More about Time

Look at the time line. Touch dot C. **(A)** That dot shows when Eric and Tom started their trip. What year was that? **(B)**

Touch dot A. **(C)** That dot shows when Eric and Tom were in the city of the future. When was that? **(D)**

Touch dot B. **(E)** That dot shows the year that Thrig was from. What year was that? **(F)**

Touch dot D. **(G)** That dot shows when Eric and Tom were in San Francisco. What year was that? **(H)**

Touch dot E. **(I)** That dot shows when Eric and Tom were in Greece. How long ago was that? **(J)**

Touch dot F. **(K)** That dot shows when Eric and Tom were in Egypt. How long ago was that? **(L)**

Touch dot G. **(M)** That dot shows when Eric and Tom saw the cave people. How long ago was that? **(N)**

A ● Eric and Tom in the city
of the future

B ● The year Thrig was from
C ● The year Eric and Tom were from
D ● Eric and Tom in San Francisco

E ● Eric and Tom in Greece
F ● Eric and Tom in Egypt

G ● Eric and Tom see cave people

C
America

In today's story, you will read about America. Here are places that are in America: Canada, the United States, Mexico, and South America.

See if you can name all those places that are in America. Ⓐ

D
Spain in 1491 Ⓐ

Tom and Eric were near an ocean. In the distance they could see an old-time sailing ship. Ⓑ There was a shack way down near the shore. Tom and Eric started down the hill toward the shack. A fat man standing next to the shack was wearing funny pants and a long robe. Ⓒ The fat man called out to Tom, but Tom couldn't understand what he said. Ⓓ Tom called, "Do you speak English?"

The man replied, "Yes."

Tom walked down to the shack. Eric followed him. Tom said, "What year is it?"

The man said, "1491."

Eric said, "Wasn't that the year that
Columbus discovered America?" ❀ 2 ERRORS ❀

"No," Tom said. "Columbus discovered
America in 1492." Ⓔ

The fat man became angry. "Did you say
Columbus?" The man pointed to the ship at the
dock. "That ship belongs to Columbus.
Columbus is a crazy person." Ⓕ

The man went into his shack. Tom and Eric
followed. On the walls were many maps, but
they did not look like any maps that Tom and
Eric had ever seen.

The man touched a spot on the largest map.

"We are here in Spain. Columbus plans to sail his ships off the end of the world. He says that the world is round, but it is flat. If the world was round, we would roll off." **G**

Eric said, "Everybody knows that the world is round."

The man shouted, "You lie. I am going to call the soldiers." **H**

Tom took out the tape recorder. Then he said to the man, "Say something. Say anything at all."

The man said, "I will take you to the soldiers."

Tom played back what the man had said. "I will take you to the soldiers."

The man looked around the room. "Who said that?" He looked at the recorder. "A voice without a man!"

Tom explained the tape recorder. Then Eric said, "That big thing on the hill is our time machine. It brought us back here in time."

The fat man shook his head. Then he said, "You know things that I do not know. Why does the world look so flat if it is round?" ①

Tom pointed to a ship that was far out on the ocean. "Look at that ship. All you can see is the top part of it." Ⓙ

The fat man looked at the ship. "You are right," he said. "I cannot see the bottom of the ship."

Tom said, "You cannot see the bottom of the ship because the earth is round: If the earth were flat, you would be able to see the whole ship. The earth looks flat because it is very, very big. You see just a small part of it." Ⓚ

Then Eric said, "Tom, I just saw something go into our time machine."

"What was it?" Tom asked.

Eric replied, "It looked like a big white dog."

The fat man hit his fist on the table. "I would like to kill that dog. He is mean. And he always comes around my shack. He bit one of my men the other day."

Eric said, "What if that dog bumps against the handle? We'll never get home." Ⓛ

Eric and Tom ran from the shack. They ran up the hill to the time machine. The fat man was right behind them. ❊ 8 ERRORS ❊

LESSON 136

1

George Washington

village

wrestle

England

president

2

Viking

crouched

disappear

whispered

hardly

3

Vocabulary words

yelp

More about Time

Look at the time line. Touch dot C.Ⓐ That dot shows when Eric and Tom started their trip. What year was that?Ⓑ

Touch dot A.Ⓒ That dot shows when Eric and Tom were in the city of the future. When was that?Ⓓ

Touch dot B.Ⓔ That dot shows the year that Thrig was from. What year was that?Ⓕ

Touch dot D.Ⓖ That dot shows when Eric and Tom were in San Francisco. What year was that?Ⓗ

Touch dot E.Ⓘ That dot shows when Columbus discovered America. What year was that?Ⓙ

Touch dot F.Ⓚ That dot shows when Eric and Tom were in Spain. What year was that?Ⓛ

Touch dot G.Ⓜ That dot shows when Eric and Tom were in Greece. How long ago was that?Ⓝ

Touch dot H.Ⓞ That dot shows when Eric and Tom were in Egypt. How long ago was that?Ⓟ

Touch dot I.Ⓠ That dot shows when Eric

and Tom saw the cave people. How long ago
was that? ⓡ

A ● Eric and Tom in the city
of the future

B ● The year Thrig was from
C ● The year Eric and Tom were from
D ● Eric and Tom in San Francisco

E ● Columbus discovered America
F ● Eric and Tom in Spain

G ● Eric and Tom in Greece

H ● Eric and Tom in Egypt

I ● Eric and Tom see cave people

C

The Dog and the Time Machine

Tom and Eric ran up the hill to the time machine. Ⓐ Tom looked inside. The big white dog was crouched down near the handle. Ⓑ

"Grrrrr," the dog said, and Tom could see his teeth. The dog was very dirty and very skinny.

Eric looked inside and then whispered, "Tom, he's right next to the handle. If he bumps into that handle, the machine will disappear and we'll never get back home."

The fat man pushed past Tom and Eric. He was holding a big stick. Ⓒ "Let me at that dog," the fat man said. "I will give him a beating he will remember." ❄ 2 ERRORS ❄

"No," Tom said and grabbed the man's arm. "Don't scare him."

The fat man looked at the inside of the time machine. He looked at the dials. He watched the lights go on and off. Suddenly, he looked very frightened. "I have never seen such a thing as this machine," he said softly. Ⓓ

Tom hardly heard what the fat man said. Ⓔ

Tom held out his hand. "Come here, boy," he said very softly.

"Grrrrrr," the dog said and showed his teeth again.

Tom turned to the fat man. "Do you have some food we can give the dog?" Tom asked.

"No, no," the man said. "I do not want to be around that dog or that machine." The man started to run back down the hill. **(F)**

Eric said, "That dog doesn't like you, Tom. Let me talk to him."

Tom stepped out of the doorway. Eric went inside and moved toward the dog very slowly. The dog crouched lower and lower as Eric moved toward him. "Don't be afraid of me," Eric said.

The dog did not show his teeth. Slowly, Eric reached out and patted him on his head. The dog's tail wagged a little. **(G)** Eric said, "You are a very nice dog."

Eric backed away from the dog. "Come here," he said softly. **(H)**

The dog stood up. His back was only a few centimeters from the handle. **(I)** Tom could hardly watch. **(J)**

"Come here," Eric said again.

The dog took another step. Then he wagged his tail. His tail banged against the handle. "Oh no," Tom said to himself.

But the dog's tail did not move the handle. The dog walked up to Eric. The dog jumped up on Eric and licked Eric's face. Ⓚ "Tom, he likes me," Eric said.

Tom patted the dog on the head. Ⓛ Then Tom looked outside the time machine. The fat man was near his shack, talking to three soldiers. The fat man pointed toward the time machine. Ⓜ

Tom said, "We'd better get out of here. Take the dog outside."

"No," Eric said. "Those men might hurt him. We've got to take him with us."

The soldiers ran up the hill. Tom ran over to the seat and sat down. Swwwwwsssssh—the door closed.

Outside, a soldier was yelling and banging on the door. BOOM, BOOM.

Eric said, "Hurry up, Tom, before he breaks the door."

BOOM, BOOM, BOOM.

Tom grabbed the handle and pulled on it. It didn't move. The dog was crouched in front of the door. "Grrrrrr," the dog growled. Tom pulled on the handle. The handle moved down.

The dials clicked and buzzed. The dog let out a little yelp. Then, as the force died down, the dog sniffed the air.

Eric said, "Tom, you pulled <u>down</u> on the handle. You should have pulled <u>up</u>."

Tom stood up and the door opened. The dog jumped back. The time machine was on another hill above water. And there was a ship down below them near the shore. The air outside was cool.

Tom pointed to the ship. "That is a Viking ship."

The Viking ship moved slowly along the shore of the ocean. Ⓡ 🏵 10 ERRORS 🏵

LESSON 137

A

1	**2**
microphone	George Washington
Saturday	president
August	England
computer	wrestle
	beard

3

Vocabulary words

1. grove of trees
2. helmet
3. village
4. huts

B

Vikings

In today's story you will read about
Vikings. Here are some facts about Vikings:

- Vikings were great fighters. Ⓐ
- Vikings sailed across the ocean to America
  before Columbus did. Ⓑ

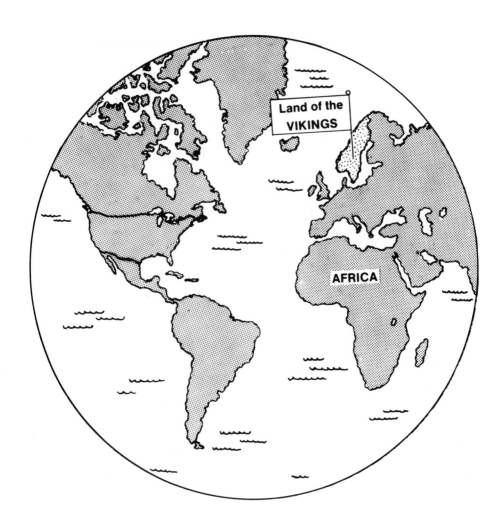

- Vikings lived far north of Italy and Spain. The map shows where the Vikings lived. Ⓒ
- The Vikings lived where the winters are very long and cold. Ⓓ

The Land of the Vikings Ⓐ

Tom and Eric were standing on the top of a hill looking at the Viking ship on the ocean below them. Tom figured that he and Eric were probably close to the year 1000. Ⓑ The Viking ship was moving slowly along the shore. Tom could hear the voices of the men on the ship as they sang. But he could not understand the words of the song. Ⓒ

As Tom watched the Viking ship, it turned and went out to sea. Eric asked, "Didn't the Vikings go to America before Columbus did?" Ⓓ

✿ 2 ERRORS ✿

Tom said, "The Vikings sailed to America long before Columbus did."

Suddenly, the dog turned around and started to growl. Ⓔ Tom turned around. A very big man was behind them. The man was dressed in a robe made of animal skins. He wore a helmet with horns on either side. Ⓕ "Grrrr," the dog growled. Ⓖ

The Viking looked at the dog and smiled. "Nur su urf," he said. Ⓗ

Tom said, "We can't understand your

language."

The Viking pointed to the dog and smiled
again. "Su urf," he said. ①

Eric said, "I think he's trying to tell us that
he likes our dog."

The Viking touched Tom's shirt. "Su urf,"

he said. Then he pointed to the time machine. Again he said, "Su urf." Ⓙ

Eric said, "I think he likes everything, Tom."

The Viking waved his hand and then pointed. "Ul fas e mern," he said.

"He wants us to come with him," Eric said.

So Tom, Eric, and the dog followed the Viking into a grove of trees. Ⓚ They walked down a hill on the other side of the grove. At last they came to a little village. There were many huts and many dogs. The dogs started to bark.

The white dog growled at the other dogs.

People came from their huts and looked at Tom and Eric. The Viking who was walking with them told the people something and the people smiled.

A big gray dog came up to Eric and Tom's dog. Suddenly, the dogs started to fight and the Vikings started to cheer. Eric said, "Tom, stop them."

Tom moved toward the dogs, but a Viking grabbed his arm and shook his head. "In sing e tool," he said. Ⓛ

The dogs continued to fight. The gray dog

was as big as the white dog, and he looked stronger than the white dog. But the white dog was a little faster. Again and again the gray dog jumped at the white dog, but the white dog got out of the way. Both dogs became tired. The white dog had a cut on his neck. The gray dog's leg was hurt. Suddenly, the gray dog stopped fighting. He was about a meter from the white dog. He was crouched down. The white dog started to move toward him, and the gray dog turned away. All the people cheered.(M) A woman ran over to the white dog. He growled at her, and everybody cheered again.(N) Then she gave him a great big bone.

Tom said, "I think our dog just beat their best dog."

Three Vikings came over and patted Tom and Eric on the back. They led Tom and Eric to a large building.(O) It was very dark inside the building.(P) There were many dogs and many tables. And it smelled bad.(Q) The Vikings sat down at one of the tables. Tom and Eric sat next to them. Then some Viking women brought in great pieces of cooked meat. Each Viking took his knife and cut off a big piece. One of the

Vikings cut pieces for Tom and Eric.

Eric said, "How are we supposed to eat? We don't have any forks." (R)

Tom pointed to the Vikings. "Just eat the way they are eating." The Vikings were eating with their hands.

Suddenly, the dogs outside began to bark again. All the Vikings stopped eating. A boy ran into the building. "Left ingra," he yelled. The Vikings grabbed their knives and ran out of the building. (S) ❈ 11 ERRORS ❈

LESSON 138

A

1	2	3
grove	computer	**Vocabulary words**
Concord	August	1. arm band
losing	microphone	2. beard
clothes	Saturday	3. wrestle
	attacked	4. fluffy

More about Time

Look at the time line. Touch dot C.Ⓐ That dot shows when Eric and Tom started their trip. What year was that?Ⓑ

Touch dot A.Ⓒ That dot shows when Eric and Tom were in the city of the future. When was that?Ⓓ

Touch dot B.Ⓔ That dot shows the year that Thrig was from. What year was that?Ⓕ

Touch dot D.Ⓖ That dot shows when Eric and Tom were in San Francisco. What year was that?Ⓗ

Touch dot E.Ⓘ That dot shows when Columbus discovered America. What year was that?Ⓙ

Touch dot F.Ⓚ That dot shows when Eric and Tom were in Spain. What year was that?Ⓛ

Touch dot G.Ⓜ That dot shows when Eric and Tom were in the Land of the Vikings. What year was that?Ⓝ

Touch dot H.Ⓞ That dot shows when Eric and Tom were in Greece. How long ago was that?Ⓟ

Touch dot I.Ⓠ That dot shows when Eric

and Tom were in Egypt. How long ago was that?Ⓡ

Touch dot J.Ⓢ That dot shows when Eric and Tom saw the cave people. How long ago was that?Ⓣ

A ● Eric and Tom in the city of the future

B ● The year Thrig was from
C ● The year Eric and Tom were from
D ● Eric and Tom in San Francisco

E ● Columbus discovered America
F ● Eric and Tom in Spain

G ● Eric and Tom in the Land of the Vikings

H ● Eric and Tom in Greece
I ● Eric and Tom in Egypt

J ● Eric and Tom see cave people

Trying to Get Home

Tom and Eric were inside the dark Viking building. Suddenly, the Vikings were fighting outside. Ⓐ The Vikings were using big, heavy swords and knives. Vikings from another village had attacked. These Vikings wore bands around their arms. Their leader was a huge man with a red beard. Ⓑ

Tom said, "I've got an idea." He held up his tape recorder and ran outside. "Stop fighting! I am the god of sounds!" he yelled.©

A Viking looked at him. "Un sur," he yelled.Ⓓ

Tom quickly played back the tape recorder.Ⓔ

Some of the Vikings stopped fighting. They looked at Tom.Ⓕ Now more Vikings stopped fighting. Tom played the recording again and again. Soon all of the Vikings were looking at Tom.Ⓖ ❋ 2 ERRORS ❋

One Viking raised his sword. His voice boomed out, "Esen trala."Ⓗ

Tom played back the Viking's voice: "Esen trala."

The Viking dropped his sword and stared at Tom. Then he turned to some of the other Vikings and said, "Su urf."Ⓘ The Vikings smiled. Then they started to laugh. They laughed and laughed. Some of them laughed so hard they almost fell over. The leader of the Vikings came over and grabbed Tom. He lifted Tom high into the air. All the Vikings held up their swords. "Sorta groob!" they shouted.

"Sorta groob!" Ⓙ

The Vikings carried Eric and Tom into the dark building. All the Vikings sat down—the Vikings from both villages. Ⓚ There was shouting and yelling and dogs barking. Everybody ate and drank. For a long time, the Vikings sang and the dogs barked.

Then the Vikings went outside. Two Vikings started to wrestle. The other Vikings cheered and the dogs barked. The two great Vikings rolled over and over on the ground.

Finally, the smaller Viking won. All the Vikings cheered. The Viking who lost stood up, smiled, and put one arm around the neck of the other Viking. Ⓛ

Later, Tom, Eric, and the dog walked back to the time machine. The Vikings followed. They sang. Some of the Vikings looked inside the time machine. Then Tom motioned so that the Vikings would move away from the time machine. Ⓜ Tom sat down in the seat. The door closed.

Eric said, "Let's try to get to our year. I'm tired of going through time." Ⓝ

Tom pushed up on the handle. Dials started

to click. Lights went on and off. Tom felt the force push against his ears. Then the force died down.

Tom stood up. The door opened. A blast of cold air came into the time machine. Outside it was snowing. The snow started to blow into the time machine.

Eric said, "Tom, let's get out of here. It's too cold out there."

Tom said, "How are we going to know where we are if we don't go outside and look around?" Ⓞ

Eric said, "But Tom, we'll freeze out there."

The time machine was on the top of a hill. The snow was coming down so hard that Tom could not see very far. He could see a grove of trees in the distance, but he couldn't see beyond. Ⓟ

Tom said, "I'll run to the grove and take a look. I'll be right back." Ⓠ

Tom ran from the time machine. He ran through the snow. It was deep and cold. His shoes filled up with snow. The cold wind cut through his shirt. Ⓡ Tom ran to the trees and looked into the distance. He didn't see anything.

But then he heard something. It sounded like a bell, very far away. So he ran through the trees toward the sound of the bell. He still couldn't see anything. And he was getting very cold. "I'd better get back to the time machine," he said to himself. He started to run back. The snow was coming down much harder now. Big fluffy flakes filled the air.

Tom ran back through the trees. Then he stopped and looked. He could not see the time machine. He called out, "Eric!" Then he listened. No answer. Tom was lost. The cold was cutting into his fingers and ears.(S) ❀ 12 ERRORS ❀

LESSON 139

A

1	2	3
George Washington	puzzle	frozen
clothes	Concord	bang
president	England	board
losing	puzzled	dashboard
		banged

4

Vocabulary words

1. valley
2. peaceful
3. lad
4. fireplace
5. English
6. march
7. spy

B **Facts about the United States**

Here are facts about things that happened when the United States became a country:

- The United States had been part of another country called England. Ⓐ

- When the United States announced that it was a country, England went to war with the United States.**(B)**
- The leader of the United States army was George Washington.**(C)**
- The United States won the war with England.**(D)**
- George Washington became the first president of the United States.**(E)**

Concord

"I must keep moving," Tom said.**(A)** He was afraid. He started running through the deep snow. He could see his breath, but no footprints.**(B)** The cold air cut through his shirt. He ran and he ran.

Suddenly, he stopped. In a valley below was a little village. There was a horse and rider moving slowly down the street. A few people were standing in front of a church. The church bell was ringing—"gong, gong, gong." The village looked very peaceful.**(C)**

Tom ran down the hill and into the village. As he came near the people who were standing in front of the church, a man said, "You should be wearing a coat." **D** ❀ 2 ERRORS ❀

Tom said, "I'm . . . lost." **E**

Another man said, "Come inside, lad."

The men took Tom into the church. Tom sat down near the fireplace in the church. The heat felt good. Tom rubbed his hands together. **F**

Slowly, the cold feeling in his hands and feet started to go away.

Tom turned to one of the men and said, "What year is it?"

The man smiled. "Everyone knows what year this is. This is 1777." ⓖ

Tom said to himself, "1777." Then he asked, "And where am I?"

"You are in the town of Concord."

Tom thought for a moment. The United States became a country in 1776. It was a year later now, and the United States was at war with England. The United States was losing the war. ⓗ

Just then, Tom heard a dog barking outside the church. ⓘ The white dog was standing in the middle of the street. Tom ran up to the dog. "Where's Eric?" Tom asked.

*The dog barked and ran down the street. ⓙ Tom started to run after him. A man caught up to Tom and said, "Here." He handed Tom a big coat. It was made of fur. Tom put it on as he ran. The coat was very warm. The man who ran with Tom was tall and skinny. He took great big steps, and Tom had trouble keeping up with him.

"My name is Robert," the man said as they ran along.

They followed the dog up a hill and down

the other side. Then they saw Eric. He was
sitting in* the snow, crying. He looked very
cold. Robert took off his coat and wrapped it
around Eric. Eric said, "I . . . I got lost." The

dog licked his face. Eric patted the dog on the head.Ⓚ

Eric, Tom, and Robert started walking back to town. Eric studied Robert's clothes and said, "We are not in the right year, are we?"Ⓛ

Tom said to Eric, "I'll tell you about the year we're in. Right now, George Washington and his army are sick and hungry. Many of them are dying."Ⓜ

Robert said, "And Washington will not be able to make it through the winter. The English are going to win the war."

"No," Tom said. "The United States will win."Ⓝ

Robert laughed. "You talk like a fool. Some of Washington's men don't have shoes. They don't have food. How can they win a battle?"

Just as Tom was going to answer Robert's question, he noticed the town below them. He could see English soldiers marching into the town. Robert said, "The English are looking for spies. If they find a spy, they shoot him."Ⓞ

Just then a shot sounded through the hills. One of the soldiers dropped to the snow. Another shot sounded. The soldiers ran this way and that way.

Robert said, "Some of Washington's men are shooting at the English."

"Kazinnnnng." Something hit a tree next to Eric. Tom said, "Hey, the English are shooting at us." Ⓟ

"Zuuuuuuump." Another shot hit the snow near Tom. Tom yelled, "Let's get out of here."

 10 ERRORS

LESSON 140

A

1	2	3
Saturday	19th	**Vocabulary words**
August	13th	1. animal tracks
banged	4th	2. puzzled
creaked	frozen	3. dashboard
		4. microphone
		5. computer

B

MORE ABOUT TIME

Look at the time line on page 439. Touch dot C. Ⓐ That dot shows when Eric and Tom started their trip. What year was that? Ⓑ

Touch dot A. Ⓒ That dot shows when Eric and Tom were in the city of the future. When was that? Ⓓ

Touch dot B. Ⓔ That dot shows the year that Thrig was from. What year was that? Ⓕ

Touch dot D. Ⓖ That dot shows when Eric and Tom were in San Francisco. What year was that? Ⓗ

Touch dot E. Ⓘ That dot shows when Eric and Tom were in Concord. What year was that? Ⓙ

Touch dot F. Ⓚ That dot shows when the United States became a country. What year was that? Ⓛ

Touch dot G. Ⓜ That dot shows when Columbus discovered America. What year was that? Ⓝ

Touch dot H. Ⓞ That dot shows when Eric and Tom were in Spain. What year was that? Ⓟ

Touch dot I. Ⓠ That dot shows when Eric and Tom were in the Land of the Vikings. What year was that? Ⓡ

Touch dot J. Ⓢ That dot shows when Eric and Tom were in Greece. How long ago was that? Ⓣ

Touch dot K. Ⓤ That dot shows when Eric and Tom were in Egypt. How long ago was that? Ⓥ

Touch dot L. ⓦ That dot shows when Eric and Tom saw the cave people. How long ago was that? ⓧ

A ● Eric and Tom in the city
      of the future

B ● The year Thrig was from
C ● The year Eric and Tom were from
D ● Eric and Tom in San Francisco
E ● Eric and Tom in Concord
F ● The United States became a country
G ● Columbus discovered America
H ● Eric and Tom in Spain
I ● Eric and Tom in the Land of the Vikings

J ● Eric and Tom in Greece

K ● Eric and Tom in Egypt

L ● Eric and Tom see cave people

C

Home Ⓐ

Tom, Eric, and Robert were running from the English soldiers. After they ran about a kilometer, Tom stopped and said, "We don't know where we're going." He turned around. "But the dog knows." Tom bent down next to the dog. "Take us back to the time machine," Tom said. Ⓑ

Tom gave the dog a little push. The dog sniffed the air and then started to run. He stopped to sniff some animal tracks. He stopped to eat snow. But then he started to run in a straight line over the hills. Ⓒ

So Tom, Eric, and Robert followed the dog. Just when Tom began to think the dog didn't know where he was going, Robert said, "What is that thing ahead of us?" Ⓓ ❉ 2 ERRORS ❉

Tom looked through the trees. "That's it. That's our time machine."

Tom, Eric, and Robert ran up to the time machine. Robert looked very puzzled. Ⓔ The time machine was filled with snow. There was so much snow inside that the seat was covered. Ⓕ Tom and Eric started to dig through the snow. They pushed most of it out of the time machine.

Then Tom turned to Robert. Tom said, "You'd better come with us. If the English soldiers find you, they'll kill you."

"No," Robert said. "I am going to fight the English. I will join Washington's army." **G**

Eric took off Robert's coat and handed it to him. "You will need this," he said.

Tom took off his coat. He said, "And you can give this to one of the other soldiers." **H**

Robert took the coats. He put one on and threw the other over his shoulder. "Good luck," he said.

Robert started running down the hill. Soon he had disappeared into the woods. Three soldiers in red coats were coming from the other direction. **I**

Tom sat down in the seat. The door did not close. **J** Tom said, "The seat must be frozen." He bounced up and down. The English soldiers were very close. The dog was standing in the doorway growling at them. One soldier came up to the doorway. "Come out of there," he yelled.

Eric pushed on the seat. Tom bounced up

and down. Suddenly, the seat creaked and—
swwwwsh—the door closed.

"Bong! Bong!" Ⓚ

"I hope the handle works," Tom said. He
pulled on the handle, but it seemed to be
frozen. Ⓛ

Tom banged on the dashboard. Suddenly, a
door opened and a microphone popped out. Ⓜ A
voice said, "What year and month do you wish
to go to?" Ⓝ

Eric and Tom looked at each other. "The

month we want is August," Eric said. Then he told the year. Ⓞ The handle moved. Several dials lit up. Ⓟ Then the voice said, "What date in August?"

Eric said, "The 19th. It is a Saturday."

Again the end of the handle moved, and several more dials lit up. Ⓠ The voice said, "What time on August 19th?"

Tom said, "Make it about the time the sun goes down."

The voice said, "What place do you wish to go to on August 19th?"

Eric described the place. Ⓡ The voice said, "On August 19th, the sun sets at 8:32 P.M. in that place."

Eric asked Tom, "Who are we talking to?"

The voice said, "I am the computer that runs this time machine." Ⓢ

Suddenly, the force pushed against Tom. Then the force died down. Ⓣ Slowly, Tom stood up.

The time machine was on the mountain where Tom and Eric had found it. Tom could see the other kids walking home down the path below. Ⓤ As Eric and Tom started down the mountain, the time machine disappeared.

"Let's get out of here," Tom said. Tom yelled out to the other kids, "Hey, wait for us!" And Tom, Eric, and the dog ran.

When they caught up to the other kids, someone asked, "Hey, where did you get the dog?"

Tom smiled. "You wouldn't believe me if I told you." Ⓥ

Another kid asked, "What's the dog's name?"

Eric said, "Columbus."

"That's a silly name for a dog," one kid said.

Eric said, "It's not a silly name for <u>this</u> dog." Ⓦ

One of the girls said, "Let's go home. We've got a long way to go."

Tom laughed. "We don't have very far to go at all." Eric laughed too. Ⓧ

"Wow!" Tom said. "It sure feels good to be home." He patted Columbus on the head. Columbus wagged his tail. The lights were going on all over the town below. That town sure looked good. Ⓨ ❀ 12 ERRORS ❀